Making Freedom

African Americans in U.S. History

SOURCEBOOK 2

⋈

A Song Full of Hope
1770–1830

OTHER BOOKS IN THIS SERIES

SOURCEBOOK 1
True to Our Native Land: Beginnings to 1770

SOURCEBOOK 3
Lift Ev'ry Voice: 1830–1860

SOURCEBOOK 4
Our New Day Begun: 1861–1877

SOURCEBOOK 5
March On Till Victory: 1877–1970

Making Freedom is a beautifully crafted five-volume sourcebook for classroom use. In its presentation of primary sources and learning strategies it has no rival in the area of African American history. This handsome, thought-provoking series belongs on the desk of every middle and high school United States history teacher who knows that without African American history there is only a partial and unbalanced United States history.

GARY B. NASH
Director, National Center for History in the Schools
University of California, Los Angeles

The Making Freedom *Sourcebooks and CDs are a treasure trove of documents, analysis, and resources guaranteed to inspire lively classroom discussion and thoughtful student research. This original collaboration between teachers and scholars offers extraordinary access to the historical and continuing role of African Americans in the shaping of our nation.*

MARILYN RICHARDSON
Former Curator, Museum of Afro-American History and
the African Meeting House, Boston, Massachusetts

Making Freedom *offers teachers of American history a powerful and compelling teaching tool to help broaden their focus curriculum. The lessons are well crafted and provide students an opportunity to sharpen historical and critical thinking skills in a dynamic, meaningful, and relevant fashion. In the hands of teachers,* Making Freedom *will make a difference.*

JIM PERCOCO
Author, Divided We Stand: Teaching
About Conflict in U.S. History

Developed through a skillful collaboration between scholars and experienced social studies teachers and curriculum specialists—and covering a span of time from medieval Jenne-Jeno to 1970—this excellent five-volume set is built around firsthand evidence (mostly written documents but also many visual materials). Undoubtedly it will be a valuable classroom resource for students and teachers alike.

ROBERT L. HALL
Department of African-American Studies
Northeastern University, Boston, Massachusetts

For many students, the fact that the past was made up of real people who made real decisions about issues that are not far different from ones that we face today rarely comes through in the textbooks that they use. Primary Source's Making Freedom *helps open the history classroom to the lives of many different types of people. The range of documents and the tips on how to use them creatively give a real opportunity for teachers to help their students understand the past and its relevance to today.*

STEVEN D. COHEN
Education Department, Tufts University

The curricula within these sourcebooks was developed by some of the most creative educators I have ever met. We are truly excited about sharing them with you.

>Rachel Zucker wrote "Paul Robeson" and "The Black Press" in Sourcebook 5

I have found as both an educator and an administrator that I have learned more of my own history by being involved in this historical project. For teachers of color, it will be most helpful in the classroom where we can share the true stories of African American culture and help to correct some misinformation of the past. After all, African American history IS American history.

>Deborah Ward contributed to "The Exodusters—Ho for Kansas!" in Sourcebook 4

I use primary sources in my curriculum because the students become more engaged in the process of discovering history for themselves. They are fascinated by reading and deciphering the art, documents, letters, diary entries, and law codes written in centuries past. I feel these exercises encourage students to empathize with people of the past and to better understand complex aspects of history. History comes alive!

>Laurel Starks wrote "The Slave Experience: Their Words and Others" and "Slavery and Resistance" in Sourcebook 3

I recall deciding in the fourth grade that history was not for me or about me. It definitely did not make me feel connected to anything. The lessons I wrote in the Primary Source Black Yankees Seminar (subsequently a part of the series) gave me an exciting rebirth experience that forged a connection for me and turned on my search for historical truth. The Making Freedom *series empowers teachers to make history come alive for students of all ages.*

>Deborah Gray wrote "Slave Literacy" and contributed to "Schooling of Free Blacks—The Roots of 'Separate But Equal'" in Sourcebook 3

I found that using these primary source materials with my students helped them understand more thoroughly the issues and complexities of the time periods being studied. Students and I use the key questions and organizing ideas to focus and guide our thinking through the many activities and assessments provided by the Sourcebooks. Students are engaged in the work and seek additional information to increase their knowledge of history.

>Leslie Kramer wrote a number of lessons in Sourcebook 1, including "Sugar and Slaves," "Riverine Craft—Bringing the Skills Over," and "Resistance and Rebellions"

Writing lessons for the Making Freedom *series represented the ideal scholarly endeavor: I could use my research and analytic skills to get to the heart of the topic and then draw on my teaching experience to present the material in a meaningful way to students. I appreciate being able to give students this opportunity to immerse themselves in the richness and subtlety of history.*

>Mark Meier wrote "Urban Disturbances" and "Many Roads to Freedom" in Sourcebook 5

Making Freedom
African Americans in U.S. History

SOURCEBOOK 2

A Song Full of Hope
1770–1830

COMPILED AND EDITED BY
THE CURRICULUM SPECIALISTS AT
PRIMARY SOURCE, INC.

FOREWORD BY
JAMES OLIVER HORTON

HEINEMANN
PORTSMOUTH, NH

Heinemann
A division of Reed Elsevier Inc.
361 Hanover Street
Portsmouth, NH 03801–3912
www.heinemann.com

Offices and agents throughout the world

© 2004 by Primary Source, Inc.

All rights reserved. No part of this book may be reproduced in any form or by any electronic or mechanical means, including information storage and retrieval systems, without permission in writing from the publisher, except by a reviewer, who may quote brief passages in a review.

Acknowledgments for borrowed material can be found on page 181.

Library of Congress Cataloging-in-Publication Data
Making freedom : African Americans in U.S. history / compiled and edited by the curriculum specialists at Primary Source, Inc. ; foreword by James Oliver Horton.
    p. cm.
  Includes bibliographical references.
  ISBN 0-325-00515-X (v. 1 : acid-free paper) — ISBN 0-325-00516-8 (v. 2 : acid-free paper) — ISBN 0-325-00517-6 (v. 3 : acid-free paper) — ISBN 0-325-00518-4 (v. 4 : acid-free paper) — ISBN 0-325-00519-2 (v. 5 : acid-free paper)
  1. African Americans—History—Study and teaching. 2. African Americans—History—Sources. I. Primary Source, Inc.

E184.7.M34 2004
973'.0496073'0071—dc22
                                                          2003024628

Editor for Heinemann: Danny Miller
Editor for Primary Source: Liz Nelson
Production service: Lisa Garboski, bookworks
Production coordinator: Vicki Kasabian
CD production: Marla Berry and Nicole Guay
Interior and cover design: Catherine Hawkes, Cat & Mouse
Typesetter: TechBooks
Manufacturing: Steve Bernier

Printed in the United States of America on acid-free paper
08 07 06 05 04 VP 1 2 3 4 5

The Making Freedom *series is dedicated to the memory of*
Clara Hicks,
*a former school principal in Newton, Massachusetts,
and a colleague at Primary Source.
She served briefly as a Project Administrator for this series
and has left us a legacy of wisdom and joy.*

Primary Source has created the Making Freedom *Sourcebooks
thanks to the generosity of these contributors:*

*National Endowment for the Humanities
Germeshausen Foundation
LEF Foundation
Massachusetts Foundation for the Humanities
Wellspring Foundation
and many individual donors*

Lift Ev'ry Voice and Sing

JAMES WELDON JOHNSON

Lift ev'ry voice and sing,
Till earth and heaven ring,
Ring with the harmonies of Liberty;
Let our rejoicing rise
High as the list'ning skies,
Let it resound loud as the rolling sea.
Sing a song full of the faith that the dark past has taught us,
Sing a song full of the hope that the present has brought us;
Facing the rising sun of our new day begun,
Let us march on till victory is won.

Stony the road we trod,
Bitter the chast'ning rod,
Felt in the days when hope unborn had died;
Yet with a steady beat,
Have not our weary feet
Come to the place for which our fathers sighed?
We have come over a way that with tears has been watered,
We have come, treading our path through the blood of the slaughtered,
Out from the gloomy past,
Till now we stand at last
Where the white gleam of our bright star is cast.

God of our weary years,
God of our silent tears,
Thou who hast brought us thus far on the way;
Thou who hast by Thy might,
Led us into the light,
Keep us forever in the path, we pray.
Lest our feet stray from the places, our God, where we met Thee,
Lest our hearts, drunk with the wine of the world, we forget Thee;
Shadowed beneath Thy hand,
May we forever stand,
True to our God,
True to our native land.

Contents

Foreword by James Oliver Horton, George Washington University xi
Project Staff xiii
Introduction xvii

CONTEXT ESSAY "Liberty and Slavery in the Era of the American Revolution" *by Robert Allison, Suffolk University* 1

Part I ✣ Meaning of Liberty

How did Revolutionary ideals affect African American expectations? How did European Americans react to these changing expectations? What legal protections did British law, colonial charters, and the Massachusetts Bill of Rights offer slaves? What references were made to slavery in the original draft of the Declaration of Independence? In what ways did individual African Americans use the courts to claim their freedom? What roles did slaves and freedmen have in the military during the Revolutionary War? How did social disruptions caused by the war lead to some southern blacks becoming British evacuees and homesteading in Canada and Sierra Leone?

LESSON 1   Human Liberation Versus the State   14
LESSON 2   African Americans in the American Revolution   26
LESSON 3   The Black Loyalists—Emigrants to a New Life   48
LESSON 4   Massachusetts Abolishes Slavery, 1783   63
LESSON 5   The Life and Times of Elizabeth "Mum Bett" Freeman, 1742–1829   73

Part II ✣ Building Community in the Post-Revolutionary Era

How did the presence of two side-by-side worlds, one enslaved and the other free, affect the development of a sense of African American community? What types of institutions did African Americans create? What role did churches play in creating community? Which existing industries provided opportunities to African Americans?

LESSON 6   Using Government Records to Locate African American Presence in Early American History *83*
LESSON 7   African Americans in the Whaling Industry *98*
LESSON 8   Leadership and Community in Philadelphia *111*

Part III ⋇ Conflict and Change

What was the significance of the correspondence between Thomas Jefferson and Benjamin Banneker? In what ways did the Haitian Revolution change perceptions of liberty among African Americans? What were the motivations behind the African colonization movement? Were proposals by African Americans for colonization in Africa a rejection of American society or an affirmation? How did the westward expansion of the Republic change the nature of slavery?

LESSON 9   Thomas Jefferson and His Responders *122*
LESSON 10   Resistance and Revolts by the Enslaved *132*
LESSON 11   Colonization: A Close Look at a Complex "Solution" *147*
LESSON 12   The Westward Expansion of Slavery and the Missouri Compromise of 1820 *163*

Glossary *177*
Credits *181*

Foreword

JAMES OLIVER HORTON
GEORGE WASHINGTON UNIVERSITY

The most exciting thing about history is the likelihood of discovery. Documents from the past—official papers, letters, diaries, newspapers, and maps—are windows into the public and private worlds of those who came before us, those who prepared the society that has shaped our lives.

The documents, lessons, and context essays in this book focus on the lives and experiences of African American people in the history of the United States. They make clear the importance of race in the formation of American culture and society. Through these documents and the interpretive essays that place them in historical context, *Making Freedom* illustrates a more inclusive American history, revealing the interracial, multicultural historical experience that Americans lived. It makes the critical point that African American history is American history made by Americans in America.

Every American has been—and continues to be—shaped by African and African American cultural heritage and its interaction with the multitude of other cultural heritages that have combined to form American culture. These documents help us to see the world of the past through the eyes of those who lived in that world and to understand the events of their time as they did. They enable us to appreciate the role of race in shaping American assumptions and expectations and understand the interconnection between the meaning of American freedom and the limitations Americans imposed on that freedom. If we are ever to have a successful conversation on race in today's society, it is essential that we come to terms with these issues.

Historical documents can bring history to life at a time when America needs a historical context for its contemporary concerns. Unfortunately, Americans are undereducated about their past, and our public school system has not successfully addressed this problem. If, as Thomas Jefferson believed, an educated citizenry is essential for the maintenance of democracy, America is in trouble.

Recent surveys make clear the critical need for better history education. The U.S. Department of Education reports that 60 percent of the nation's high school seniors cannot demonstrate even a fundamental knowledge of U.S. history. This ignorance is especially glaring on the subject of race. More than half of the students could not identify Africa as the continent from which people were brought to be enslaved in the Western Hemisphere. Almost two-thirds could not correctly identify the term "Jim Crow" as the set of laws that enforced racial segregation, and less than one quarter could explain the purpose of the Fifteenth Amendment as a Constitutional protection against discrimination in voting, even when the wording of the amendment was provided to them.

If there was ever a time to enhance history education, that time is now. The documents in this book do just that, and the accompanying lesson plans suggest effective teaching strategies. From first-hand accounts of the Atlantic slave trade, to descriptions of black seafaring communities after the Revolution, to the wartime experiences of black Civil War soldiers, to the emergence of the Harlem Renaissance, *Making Freedom* presents a compelling and dramatic American story. It introduces the major concerns and events of the African American experience and the significance of race in America. These documents transport students back in time and allow them to discover the past in its own words and on its own terms.

Standard history textbooks provide information about the past that is important, but too often less than engaging. These documents and lessons are as lively and interesting as the human struggles they portray. Whereas textbooks frequently separate African Americans from the general American experience, *Making Freedom* places African American history at the center of the broad sweep of national history.

Most important, it helps us to evaluate America's past through a reading of direct historical evidence. Students will come to understand history through their personal investigation. This critical component of learning can add excitement and meaning to the educational experience. Students become more than simply consumers of historical information. They move closer to being historians and begin to understand the excitement of historical discovery.

Most of us who have become professional historians remember the moment when history became something more than a list of names and events, when it became an adventurous search for meaning. At the moment when facts become not simply significant in themselves but inspiring bits of evidence to be used in building a case for historical interpretation, we started to feel like real historians, detectives on the trail of history.

When students feel like historical detectives they will have less trouble remembering the significant fundamentals of history and they will appreciate the importance of the past.

Those who understand how exciting history is and understand its meaning for the present and the future never find it boring. Instead, they become lifelong learners of history. The documents in *Making Freedom* open a new and exciting world of the past and provide a greater appreciation of the full range of American history and of the lives of the people who made it.

Project Staff

Primary Source Staff

Anna Roelofs, Project Director
Kathy Bell, Librarian
Renee Covalucci, Picture Research
Abby Detweiler, Program Associate
Jim Diskant, Curriculum Specialist
Kathleen M. Ennis, Executive Director
Betty Hillmon, Kodaly Music Consultant
Eve Lehmann, Permissions Editor
Roberta Logan, Education Director
Rachel Margolis, Program Associate
Brande Martin, Program Associate
Charles Rathbone, Board of Directors
Jesse Ruskin, Music Researcher
Kelly Scott, Program Associate
Martha Shethar, Photo Researcher
Ann Vick-Westgate, Editor

Interns

Lucia Carballo
Kendra Carpenter
Jessica Kyle Ellis
Mike Fearon
Tracey Graham, Mellon Fellow
Imani Hope
Meredith Katter
Nina Miller
Sam Schwartz

Special thanks to James Jones of Northeastern University for his musical expertise, to Marvin Karp, Benjamin Kendall, Jill Minot-Seabrook, and Anthony Parker for their advice, to The Lovejoy Society, DeKalb, Illinois; and to Pam Matz, librarian at Harvard University.

Advising Scholars

Frances Smith Foster, Emory University
V. P. Franklin, Columbia University Teachers' College (Evaluator)
Paul Gagnon, Emeritus, Boston University
Gerald Gill, Tufts University
Robert Hall, Northeastern University
Emmett Price, Northeastern University
Heather Cox Richardson, Suffolk University
John Ross, National Center of Afro-American Artists, Boston

Contributing Scholars

Robert Allison, Suffolk University
Edmund Barry Gaither, Museum of the National Center for African American Artists, Boston
Robert Hayden, Independent Scholar
Betty Hillmon, Park School
James Oliver Horton, George Washington University
Lois Horton, George Mason University
Grey Osterud, Historian
Patrick Rael, Bowdoin College
Marilyn Richardson, Independent Scholar
Julie Richter, Independent Scholar

Teacher-Authors

Wendell Bourne, Cambridge Public Schools
Phyllis Bretholtz, Teacher/Educational Consultant
Ilene Carver, Boston Public Schools
Monny Cochran, Weston Public Schools
Julie Craven, Cambridge Public Schools
Andrea Doremus Cuetara, Boston Public Schools
Inez Dover, Newton Public Schools
Kathleen Drew, Cambridge Public Schools
Sharon Fleming, Abington Public Schools
Linda Forman, Framingham Public Schools
Richard Berry Fulton, Boston Public Schools
Deborah Gray, Community Educator

Andrea Gross, Westwood Public Schools
Jennifer Hames, Boston Public Schools
Deborah Hood-Brown, Cambridge Public Schools
Leslie Kramer, Cambridge Public Schools
Roberta Logan, Boston Public Schools
Peter Lowber, Malden Public Schools
Mark Meier, University of Virginia
Nicole Miller, Westborough Public Schools
Martin Milne, Eaglebrook School, Deerfield
Edward Morrison, Winthrop Public Schools
Melisa Nasella, Lincoln-Sudbury Public Schools
Karl Netter, Boston Public Schools
Catherine O'Connor, Newton Country Day School
Alexandria Pearson, Metro Director, Natick High School
Gwynne Alexandra Sawtelle, Westborough Public Schools
Andrew Shen, Lincoln-Sudbury Public Schools
Laurel Starks, Milton Academy
Sandra Stuppard, Boston Public Schools
Deborah Ward, Wellesley Public Schools
Joseph Zellner, Concord Public Schools
Rachel Zucker, Burlington Public Schools

Introduction

Making Freedom: African Americans in U.S. History grew out of the synergy and vision of a group of Boston-area teachers, several scholars, and the program staff of Primary Source. Beginning in 1995 with a series of seminars on "Black Yankees" of the eighteenth and nineteenth centuries, the project grew and expanded to reach across the country and over time, up to the last quarter of the twentieth century.

Fortunately for all of us who see history as discovery, continuing scholarship is illuminating almost four centuries of African American thought, creativity, and activism in the social, political, and cultural development of our nation. Although work has been going on for years at the university level to understand the ways in which African American ideas and experiences influenced the development of our national culture and political ideology, little of this new thinking has yet become part of the standard school curriculum. The traditional historical narrative forming the basis of content for precollege students often relegates the study of African American history to separate units on slavery or to the struggle for civil rights. *Making Freedom* offers precollegiate teachers and their students exposure to exciting and informed scholarship on 400 years of history, thus strengthening the content and adjusting the lens through which African American history is viewed and understood.

The *Making Freedom* sourcebooks contain information and materials that demonstrate at least two important phenomena: the social agency and intellectual achievement shown throughout African American history from the colonial period forward and the inextricable relationship of African Americans to the collective history and cultural development of the United States. The primary sources contained in these sourcebooks reveal a diversity of perspectives and experiences among African Americans from their first arrival in British North America. In contemporary textbooks, slavery is often presented as a singular experience that shaped the character of all African Americans. *Making Freedom* intentionally illuminates the variety of the slave experience for African Americans, focusing both on individual ideas and actions and on collective efforts to hold America accountable to the ideals of freedom and equality.

Through the speeches and writings of scholars and activists, slave narratives, poetry, fiction, music, and fine arts, revealing agency in the face of repression,

Making Freedom illumines the ways in which Africans and African Americans have influenced American thought and cultural expression, as well as our traditions of freedom and democracy.

Making Freedom:

- ❖ provides teachers with multidisciplinary scholarship, primary source materials, and lesson plans concerning African American history from fourteenth-century Africa through the Civil Rights Movement of the 1970s
- ❖ presents this new material in ways that stimulate teachers and students to ask questions about how the intellectual history of African Americans relates to mainstream history and provokes a deeper understanding of the achievements and frustrations of African Americans in the pursuit of a lived freedom
- ❖ inspires teachers, who in turn inspire students, to become active learners, engaged in the process of historical research and community exploration, to tolerate both conflict and ambiguity in the historical narrative, and to learn more about themselves and others in an increasingly complex, pluralistic world
- ❖ addresses a variety of issues—scholarship, teaching strategies, and diverse student preparations for understanding history—and pulls them all together into a useful resource
- ❖ increases understanding and teaching capacity of both experienced and novice teachers for presenting the powerful and integral role of African American intellectual history in American history

The history of minorities *is* American history—to leave it out or mention it peripherally deprives students and teachers alike, giving an incomplete and often a false view of our past. Both majority and minority students gain from learning a more holistic story. Because mainstream history is often restricted to the story of one dominant group, complicating what is taught as history becomes a vital and legitimate goal for anyone seriously concerned with historical accuracy.

How This Series Was Created

In the summer of 1998, with financial support from the National Endowment for the Humanities, an enthusiastic group of teachers and scholars met to imagine and then to begin to create a multipart series of curriculum sourcebooks. We formed into working groups, each with a scholar, teachers, and a curriculum specialist.

Since its inception, the project has been informed by emerging scholarship in African American history and the growing availability of primary source materials to the general public. History has been described as a funnel—lots of stories go in, but only a few emerge to be told. Our goal is to enlarge the mainstream narrative for teachers and students, offering an inclusive history that places African Americans among the founders and shapers of our culture. *Making Freedom* uncovers stories of African American agency and intellectual vision and demonstrates how this intellectual history catalyzed movements such as abolition and civil rights and contributed to new interpretations of the Constitution. Recognizing that some of the primary source testimony of African Americans is in nonliterary form, primary source documents may be in the form of original artworks and musical scores that illustrate African American contributions to the development of American art, folk culture, and religious traditions.

Although one major thrust of this curriculum initiative is related to content, there are pedagogical objectives as well. Teachers and students need tools and strategies to enable the process of discovery and to encourage investment in learning. By using these sourcebooks, teachers can help their students become active participants in history. Through reading firsthand, authentic accounts of moments in history, looking at an engraving or listening to a piece of music, students are moved to ask questions and learn to formulate their own opinions about a person, an issue, or an event.

As we designed *Making Freedom* and began to draft materials, we drew heavily upon James Banks' paradigm for transforming curriculum. Banks' model shifts the perspective away from a conventionally focused study to reveal a more inclusive and far more interesting array of interrelated content. Offering a variety of activities and nontextbook, original source material, this approach lays the groundwork for teachers to transform their teaching goals and methods.

Who We Are

Primary Source, a teacher resource center in Watertown, Massachusetts, promotes education in the humanities that is historically accurate, culturally inclusive, and explicitly concerned with ethical issues such as racism and other forms of discrimination. Its services link university and school and combine scholarly research from original sources with practical knowledge of how adults and students learn. Through institutes, seminars, and conferences, Primary Source models an active, interdisciplinary approach to teaching. Primary Source offers educators intellectual enrichment and opportunities to participate in serious, professional dialogue with scholars and other classroom teachers.

Primary Source supports teachers' efforts to restructure their social studies teaching by serving as a conduit for primary source materials that reveal the voices of people from various ethnic, racial, and cultural groups within the United States and from countries around the world. Once these original source documents are brought to light and their intellectual and creative accomplishments are revealed, curriculum content is necessarily more inclusive of both genders and all racial and ethnic groups. Students may then see themselves in the curriculum and feel more connected to the educational process, to a cultural past, and to a civic future.

Using Primary Sources

The organization Primary Source takes its name from the same term used by historians to distinguish original, uninterpreted material from secondary or third-hand accounts. Thus a photograph, a memoir, or a letter is a primary source; an essay interpreting the photograph or memoir is usually, though not always, a secondary source. A textbook, still further removed, is a tertiary source.

In some instances, the same document or other piece of evidence may be a primary source in one investigation and secondary in another. For example, Henry Wadsworth Longfellow's poem "Paul Revere's Ride" is a primary source when it is considered as a reflection of how nineteenth-century citizens romanticized the Revolutionary War. It is not, however, a primary source that provides information about the events of April 18–19, 1775. (Paul Revere never did arrive in Concord.)

Making Freedom utilizes a range of primary sources. Included are maps, travel journals, letters, illustrations, engravings and other kinds of art, business records, diaries, wills, autobiographies, contemporary biography, advertisements (including those for the sale or recapture of slaves), music (including folk songs), and photographs of artifacts.

Although it is imperative to read secondary sources in order to understand context and background, introducing students to "the real stuff" raises student interest and curiosity and offers opportunities for students to make discoveries on their own. The closer students get to real people's lives, the better chance they have to formulate real questions and to care about people and events from another time and place. In a March 2002 speech to members of the Boston Athenaeum, historian David McCullough advised, "To understand the people of a particular historical period, you have to read what they read, not just what they wrote. You have to listen to the music, look at the paintings . . . ."

When textbooks are used as the only source of information, it is much more difficult for students to take ownership, both of their own learning and of a particular body of knowledge. It is very difficult to remember other people's generalizations or conclusions. Original source material provides students with rich opportunities for inquiry, the chance to move from concrete to abstract thinking and back again.

Teaching About Race

In the 1990s, a national dialogue about race was initiated by the Clinton administration. This endeavor was not widely covered in the media, and it is difficult to assess what was accomplished. The creators of this series believe that in order to bring about healing of a shameful national past, a dialogue about race needs to begin at the classroom level and be carried out into the world by students grounded in an honest study of history and committed to social justice.

We Are All Involved

The seeds of ignorant, biased, and racist opinions and feelings are often sown in children as they grow up, through families, the media, friendships, and even schools and religious institutions. Although students are not to blame for bringing ignorant opinions into the classroom, we must all now be accountable for attitudes and actions we take into the future. Discussions of racism often focus on blacks and other people of color as victims, essentially making it a black problem. The question of racism's cost to white people is rarely raised. Yet racism presents a serious challenge to any individual's ability to reason, make sound judgments, and develop perspective.

Individual Discovery

In studying the racial history of this country, we see that many painful things have happened in the past and continue to happen today in many communities. In general, students lack accurate information, ways to analyze this information as well as their own feelings and experiences, and an ability to articulate their analysis. Our job as teachers and students is to uncover the prejudices that exist in our institutions, our culture, and ourselves and to revisit our history in a careful, inclusive, and truthful manner. As a more accurate understanding of our complicated racial history is achieved, students can express their new knowledge in a variety of ways, as the activities in the lessons suggest. Finally, they can be encouraged to take action to address issues of unfairness in their schools and communities.

Depending on the composition of the class, there may be students who feel particularly vulnerable or targeted by the material discussed on a given day. Typically, students of color become angry and aggressive, while white students feel guilty and defensive. In addition, students who are of mixed race may feel conflicted. All students should be encouraged to express their thoughts and feelings; students learn a great deal from each other.

Giving students ample time to reflect in writing on what they have learned is a good outlet for feelings and is also a way to discover a student who may be having an especially difficult time. A piece of private reflective writing may reveal conflicts appropriate for the whole class to discuss or individual conflicts that need to be responsibly addressed by the teacher.

Class Discussion

Students seldom have the opportunity to engage in critical, analytical discussions about race. Our role as educators is to provide them with the information and tools to do so constructively. Students can be engaged in setting class guidelines for discussion of controversial subjects. Some examples follow.

1. All opinions and expressions of feelings and emotions are accepted and respected in class, whether other students share them or not.
2. Opinions and feelings expressed on sensitive topics should be kept within the confines of the classroom, not discussed elsewhere.
3. Students should speak from their own experience, using "I-statements" as much as possible. This simply means that students should start with, "I think, I heard, I believe, I feel . . ." rather than "You're wrong because . . ." The former prompts reflection, whereas the latter can feel like a direct attack on another speaker.
4. Students should know also that it is fine to choose *not* to speak.

How to Use This Book

Making Freedom is intended for use as a resource in all American history classes at the middle and high school levels. This series enables teachers to weave the African American story into and throughout the wider narrative. We have purposely emphasized individuals and events that are not often included in standard American history textbooks. Our purpose is to widen and deepen the narrative, not to repeat the few names and incidents already familiar to most teachers and students.

The five *Making Freedom* curriculum sourcebooks provide innovative, intellectually compelling curriculum materials that fit into the conventional scope and sequence. The sourcebooks specifically examine the African American intellectual tradition in the context of the following historical eras: (1) Colonial America; (2) Revolution and Forging the Nation; (3) Antebellum Reform; (4) Civil War and Reconstruction; and (5) The Gilded Age into the Twentieth Century. The five sourcebooks, with titles from "Lift Ev'ry Voice and Sing" by James Weldon Johnson, are:

True to Our Native Land: Beginnings to 1770

A Song Full of Hope: 1770–1830

Lift Ev'ry Voice: 1830–1860

Our New Day Begun: 1861–1877

March On Till Victory: 1877–1970

Each book contains the following:

- a table of contents for the series
- one or two context essays written by scholars
- lesson plans, including primary sources
- a glossary

The accompanying CD-ROM includes all primary source materials, supplementary materials, and a time line and annotated bibliography for the entire series.

Each lesson contains

- Introduction
- Organizing Idea
- Student Objectives
- Key Questions
- Primary Source Materials
- Vocabulary
- Student Activities
- Further Student and Teacher Resources
- Contemporary Connections

Several lessons also include music selections.

Together, the **context essays** at the beginning of each book and the **introductions** to individual lessons provide background information necessary for understanding the primary sources and engaging in the activities. Teachers can use this introductory material in a variety of ways. For example, they can have the students read the introductions in their entirety, present the information in a brief lecture, create background information sheets with key points, or ask students working in groups to research the answers to questions that create a context for the lesson.

Vocabulary lists with topical words are included, and the words are defined in the **glossary**. In many instances, given the historical period of the documents, additional vocabulary lists are provided under supplementary materials to help students better understand what they read.

Each lesson includes a variety of teaching strategies designed to engage student interest. Suggested **activities** include study and analysis of primary sources, mapping, research and writing, debating, creating graphic displays, and role-plays that involve assumption of a particular perspective, sometimes an unpopular or (in the twenty-first century) an unacceptable one. This activity needs to be understood as an attempt to see things as they were in a particular time in the past. The challenge is to try not to view all events from the perspective and values of today. When an activity calls for speculation or analysis, it is important to have verifying information available close at hand—in the classroom, the school library, or online. A speculation exercise is not a standalone activity, but, together with research to clarify information and verify a theory, it gives students the opportunity to act as historians.

Because the context essays and lessons were written by a group of scholars and teachers, they offer a variety of writing and instructional approaches. Although the format for all the lessons is the same, we have respected the authors' voices and have not edited them to a uniform length or style. The lessons vary in length and level of detail and offer a choice of activities.

We would not expect teachers to use every activity in every lesson. Rather, they should choose those lessons—and, within the lessons, those activities—that dovetail best with their instructional plan and meet the needs and learning styles of their students. We have set out a buffet—we do not intend for all of it to be consumed by each teacher.

A list of **further resources** is provided with most lessons. Although every effort has been made to ensure that references to websites are current, they do change. Teachers may wish to check URLs before giving students assignments. Students should also be cautioned to evaluate information found in a website carefully, checking who is the author and who sponsors the site.

Each lesson includes a **contemporary connection**. Our intent is to demonstrate that the issues raised by studying the primary sources do not pertain only to the past. Some remain the same; others have been transmuted a little. This feature gives resources and often asks open-ended questions for further exploration.

Some of the **primary source materials** are difficult for students to read. They have been set in type, but no changes have been made to the original language. As a result, the documents contain syntax with which students may not be familiar, as well as vocabulary no longer in active use or for which meaning has shifted. Sometimes words are spelled differently. Each teacher knows best how to adapt a lesson to students' skill levels. The books include suggestions, such as having students work in pairs or small groups, reading the documents aloud to the class, and/or providing vocabulary definitions before students tackle the documents.

The lengthier documents have been abbreviated in the sourcebooks. All **primary source materials** appear in full on the accompanying CD-ROMs and can be printed out for classroom use.

This *Adinkra* symbol represents the Akan belief that we must look at and learn from the past in order to move with wisdom into the future. It teaches people to value and protect their cultural heritage.

Liberty and Slavery in the Era of the American Revolution

ROBERT ALLISON

I. Slavery and Liberty

When his owner brought enslaved African American James Somerset with him from Massachusetts to England in 1771, Somerset took the opportunity to escape. His owner recaptured him and decided to punish Somerset by selling him to a Jamaican sugar plantation. Slavery in Massachusetts was a hardship; in Jamaica, it was practically a death sentence. Somerset contacted Granville Sharp, an English philanthropist who had begun a one-man crusade against slavery. Sharp helped Somerset sue for his freedom. Slavery, he argued, violated natural law, and a man could only be held as a slave if Parliament expressly permitted it. The "air of England is too pure for a slave to breathe," Somerset's lawyers argued. After many delays, and after privately urging Parliament to make some positive law protecting slavery, in June 1772 England's highest court ruled in Somerset's favor. The law of Massachusetts, and of all other of Britain's colonies, might recognize James Somerset as property, but the law of England recognized him only as a person.

Another slave in Massachusetts, Phillis Wheatley, wrote in 1774 that "in every human Breast, God has implanted a Principle, which we call Love of Freedom. . . ." This principle was the root of both the *Somerset* decision and of an argument between the American colonies and the British parliament. Leaders in the American colonies argued that Parliament could not tax the people of the American colonies, nor regulate their trade, without their consent. To do so would deprive these people of their fundamental right to govern themselves. To make these people subject to Parliamentary power would deprive them of their liberty, and make them slaves.

The Massachusetts Assembly had led the American struggle against Parliament's power to tax. Concurrently, four Massachusetts slaves, Peter Bestes, Sambo Freeman, Felix Holbrook, and Chester Joie, in 1773 petitioned the Assembly on behalf of their "fellow slaves in this Province" praising the leaders for their strong stand against arbitrary power. "We expect great things from men who have made such a noble stand against the designs of their fellow men to enslave them." The four slaves asked the assembly to consider their "deplorable state" and provide the relief which "as men, we have a natural right to...." How could the Assembly, so boldly asserting the natural rights of men, deprive some men and women of liberty? British author Samuel Johnson, dismissing American grievances against Parliament, asked, "How is it that we hear the loudest yelps for liberty from the drivers of Negroes?"

Slavery was central to the American economy, so central it makes us wonder why the leaders of the American opposition introduced the idea of universal liberty into their argument. More than twenty percent of the American population were enslaved Africans or African Americans. In Virginia and Maryland, the Assemblies resolved to end the slave trade as part of their resistance to British imperialism. Those Chesapeake colonies, producers of tobacco, were home to more than half of the slaves in North America. In fourteen of Virginia's thirty-nine counties blacks were a majority, and in parts of South Carolina's rice-producing low country, blacks formed ninety percent of the population.

Slavery and the slave trade were vital to each colonial economy. New England ships were among those bringing slaves from Africa to the New World in increasing numbers—an average of 60,000 slaves were brought to the Americas every year in the 1750s and 1760s. While the overwhelming number of Africans were landed on the sugar islands of the West Indies, the ports of Boston, Newport, New London, New York and Philadelphia thrived by sending food and supplies to feed the West Indian slave population and refining the sugar brought back in return.

The slave trade was also becoming a driving force in England's economy. After 1750, Britain's Royal African Company had taken over much of the African slave trade. While this gave England the economic benefit, it also gave England the considerable moral problem of profiting from the traffic in slaves. Philadelphia Quaker Anthony Benezet wrote *An Account of Guinea* in 1766, showing the history and cultural achievements of the people of West Africa, and condemning the slave trade as a moral crime. His *Caution and Warning to Great Britain and her Colonies* (1767) condemned slavery and the slave trade. In Philadelphia, Benezet opened a school for black children, showing that when given the opportunity, they were as capable of learning as any other children. In England, philanthropist Granville Sharp reprinted Benezet's pamphlets, and in Philadelphia Benezet reprinted Sharp's pamphlet, *The Injustice and Dangerous Tendency of Tolerating Slavery* (1769). Both men encouraged John Wesley, founder of Methodism, to write his own *Thoughts on Slavery* in 1774.

Sharp believed that the American colonial assemblies should be empowered to end slavery and that they should resist Parliament's attempts to constrain them. The American colonies in the early 1770s moved against the slave trade, as part of their general campaign against British trade policies. The assemblies adopted nonimportation, but colonial governors, who represented royal authority, vetoed these measures. Only Parliament, the governors insisted, could regulate American trade. But by including an attack on the slave trade in their grievances against British policy, the assemblies heartened those seeking to abolish the slave trade (called "abolitionists"). Pennsylvania reformer Benjamin Rush predicted in 1773 that the "emancipation of slaves in America will now be attended with but few difficulties except such as arise from instructions given to our Governors not to favor laws made for that purpose." Rush and other Americans blamed the British for perpetuating slavery in America. But slavery was being weakened and would be swept away by the "spirit of liberty and religion with regard to the poor Negroes," which was "spreading rapidly through the country."

II. *England and American Slaves*

The spirit of liberty did not spread as rapidly among white Americans as Rush had predicted. It did, however, stir in a different way among American slaves. James Madison, recently returned from Princeton to his family's plantation in Virginia, wrote to his friend William Bradford (a Philadelphia printer) in 1774 that some slaves in his neighborhood were conspiring to join the King's forces and win their freedom when war came. From Philadelphia, Bradford reported to Madison that a London correspondent told of a British plan to declare "all Slaves & Servants free that would take arms against the Americans." Henry Muhlenberg, Philadelphia Lutheran minister, reported that slaves "secretly wished that the British army might win, for then all Negro slaves will gain their freedom."

In November 1775, Virginia's royal governor, Lord Dunmore, offered freedom to any slave who joined the Crown and resisted a rebel master. Many did. Dunmore raised a regiment of black soldiers in Virginia. In 1775 the Dorchester County, Maryland, Committee of Inspection reported increasing "insolence" among blacks, and seized eighty guns, swords, and bayonets that the slaves had concealed. Thousands of former slaves left South Carolina with the British forces when the war ended, going to Canada or England, and bringing South Carolina's slave population down from 104,000 in 1775 to 80,000 in 1782. Thomas Jefferson, whose plantation the British raided while he was governor (he was nearly captured; many of his slaves were taken by the British) estimated that 30,000 Virginia slaves ran off during the war. Slaves enlisting in the British army and running away from owners weakened the American cause. But slaves could also threaten the American cause by staying at home, acting as spies and transmitting information, or organizing rebellions of their own. A South Carolina delegate to Congress objected to having slaves counted for purposes of taxation since slaves were property, and for tax purposes there was no difference between a slave and a sheep. In response, Benjamin Franklin observed that "Slaves rather weaken than strengthen the state, and therefore there is some difference between them and sheep: sheep will never make any insurrections."

Had the British used slavery against the Americans, the war certainly would have ended differently. But the British did not. Why not? The British were fighting to preserve the empire, and much of the empire's wealth was produced by slave labor. Attack slavery in South Carolina and Virginia, and you threaten it in Barbados and Jamaica. Free the slaves of rebels in Virginia, and you threaten the loyalists there. Britain fought to preserve the colonial system, which depended on slavery, not to destroy it.

III. "All men created equal"

On the other hand, the Americans had based their claim to independence on the idea that "all men are created equal." American slaveowners and American slaves had made a commitment to liberty and equality. But did this commitment mean the same thing to an American slave as it did to an American slaveholder?

As Jefferson was drafting the Declaration of Independence, back in Virginia planter and statesman George Mason was working on a Constitution for that state. Mason understood that the purpose of government was to protect the rights of individuals, so his Constitution began with a Declaration of Rights. The Declaration began by saying that "All men are born equally free and independent and have certain inherent natural Rights, of which they cannot by any Compact, deprive or divest their posterity. . . ." The other members of Virginia's Assembly balked at this. What would this mean to Virginia's slaves if they were declared to be free and equal, and to have natural rights? The Assembly made a careful amendment. "All men, <u>when they entered into a state of society</u>, had rights of which they could not be divested." Thus, the Virginians could argue that the Africans they enslaved had not been in a state of society, and that they had agreed to their own enslavement. According to this tortured formulation, people in a civilized society could not agree to give up their natural rights, but those outside of society could do so.

Thomas Jefferson's draft of the Declaration of Independence, after stating the fundamental precept that all men are created equal and have inalienable rights and that governments exist to secure these rights, listed the acts of the British government that were intended to destroy the rights of the colonists. Jefferson's final charge against the King was that he had "waged cruel war against human nature itself, violating its most sacred rights of life & liberty in the persons of a distant people who never offended him, captivating & carrying them into slavery in another hemisphere, or to incur miserable death in their transportation thither." He blasted the King for this "piratical warfare" and for keeping "open a market where MEN should be bought & sold. . . ." Jefferson ended this philippic against the King's "assemblage of horrors" and this "execrable commerce" with a charge showing the ambivalence of the American cause: "He is now exciting those very people to rise in arms among us, and to purchase that liberty of which <u>he</u> has deprived them, by murdering the people upon whom <u>he</u> has . . . obtruded them; thus paying off former crimes committed against the <u>liberties</u> of one people, with crimes which he urges them to commit against the <u>lives</u> of another."

Congress struck this whole passage from the Declaration. The colonists had cut off the slave trade as part of their boycott of British goods, but South Carolina and Georgia would not renounce the trade for all time. And other delegates worried about the moral inconsistency in the charge that the King alone was responsible for slavery or the slave trade, or the final suggestion that the slaves would not have cause to rise up against their masters without the King's provocation. Though Congress expunged this attack on slavery from the Declaration, the rhetoric of liberty and equality remained intact. These ideas continued to form the basic idea for the purpose of government in the new nation.

In 1780, Massachusetts adopted a new Constitution, written by John Adams. The Massachusetts Constitution began with a Declaration of Rights, nearly identical with the Virginia Constitution proposed four years earlier by Mason. All men are born free and have certain inherent rights of which they cannot be divested. To Quok Walker, a slave in Worcester County, and Elizabeth Freeman, a slave in Berkshire County, these words meant that no person in Massachusetts could be a slave. Freeman (1781) and Walker (1783) took their cases to court. Levi Lincoln, a Worcester lawyer (who later served as Attorney General of the United States in Jefferson's administration) argued Walker's case. The presiding judge, William Cushing (whom George Washington later appointed to the U.S. Supreme Court) told the jury in Walker's case that "the idea of slavery is inconsistent with our own conduct and Constitution." While slavery had long been practiced in America and elsewhere, Cushing noted that "a different idea has taken place with the people of America, more favorable to the natural rights of mankind, and that natural, innate desire of Liberty with which Heaven (without regard to color, complexion, or shape of noses) has inspired all the human race." Slavery, Cushing said, was inconsistent with the Massachusetts's Constitution's declaration "that all men are born free and equal—and that every subject is entitled to liberty, and to have it guarded by the laws, as well as life and property." When the first U.S. census was taken in 1790, Massachusetts was the only state not to record any slaves.

Cushing noted a changed spirit in America, as the idea of liberty had taken on new meaning and importance. Pennsylvania adopted a gradual emancipation law in 1780, declaring all persons born on or after March 1, 1780, to be free. The children of all people in slavery before March 1, 1780, would be free on reaching the age of 28. Rhode Island and Connecticut adopted similar emancipation laws in 1784, and New York in 1799. These laws did not free slaves immediately. A slave born in Pennsylvania on February 28, 1780, could remain a slave until he or she died, and in New Jersey, where a gradual emancipation law passed in 1804, there would still be slaves at the time of the Civil War. But gradual emancipation designed to "compensate" slaveowners for their "property" was a first step, and even in Virginia and Maryland, which rejected gradual emancipation proposals, the legislatures made it easier for owners to free their slaves. The number of free blacks in the Chesapeake region grew throughout the Revolutionary period, so that by 1810 one third of the country's free blacks lived in Virginia and Maryland, more than in any other region.

IV. Blacks in the American Army

When George Washington arrived in Cambridge to take command of the Continental forces in 1775, he was disturbed to find white and black soldiers sharing the same camp. Black soldiers had fought in every engagement: at Lexington and

Concord, and at Bunker Hill, where Peter Salem was credited with killing British major John Pitcairn. But Washington wanted to keep blacks out of the Continental army, and though his policy was adopted, he shortly had to reverse it as he could not refuse to allow willing men to serve. Rhode Island's black regiment fought with distinction at Newport, and Connecticut's black troops were under the nominal command of one of Washington's chief aides. In 1779 Washington dispatched John Laurens to his native South Carolina to raise a black regiment, giving the soldiers "their freedom with their muskets," in the words of Alexander Hamilton. However, South Carolina's legislature refused to allow Laurens to raise this regiment.

Despite the ambivalence, or even resistance, of some whites, black men did join the American forces. Liberty, equality, and freedom took on a deeply personal meaning for many of these soldiers. Of three hundred black men known to have served in Connecticut's military force, eighteen gave their last name as either "Freedom" or "Freeman", and five others called themselves "Liberty." Free black James Forten, son of a Philadelphia sail-maker, and a former pupil of Anthony Benezet, enlisted on an American privateer. When he was captured at sea, the son of the British captain befriended the fifteen-year-old Forten. The friendship led the captain to offer Forten free passage to England. "NO! NO!" Forten replied. "I am here a prisoner for the liberties of my country; I never, NEVER, shall prove a traitor to her interests." Forten, along with other captured Americans, spent the rest of the war on a British prison ship in New York harbor.

In the early years of the republic, when black men like Forten fought for the revolutionary cause, Congress and other political leaders took steps toward fulfilling the promise of liberty. The Continental Congress adopted the Northwest Ordinance in 1787, barring slavery north of the Ohio River after 1800, and the Constitution, which went into effect in 1789, gave Congress the power to end the slave trade in 1807. But additional attempts to spur broader emancipation, or to protect the rights of free black people, sputtered and failed.

It may have seemed to African Americans that their chances for liberty would have been better under the British crown. Prince Hall, a free man from Barbados, who had petitioned the Massachusetts assembly on behalf of his neighbors in slavery, served in the Revolutionary army, and after the war wanted to form a Masonic lodge. Hall saw the benefit Masonic brotherhood had in fostering community bonds, but was not permitted to join any of the Boston lodges. He sought to charter a lodge that would admit blacks, but again was refused. So Hall sent to England for a charter, which was granted in 1787.

By the end of the war, James Allen, born a slave in Philadelphia, and Absalom Jones, born a slave in Delaware, had become free and, through hard work and talent, became leaders in the black community. Allen became a Methodist preacher, and in 1786 began preaching to blacks every Sunday morning at 5 A.M. so he would not interfere with services for whites. Just as Hall had been shut out of the Masons, an organization seeking universal brotherhood, Jones and Allen saw the line drawn between themselves and other Methodists. In 1787, they and other Philadelphia

African Americans formed the Free African Society, a nondenominational meeting place for Philadelphia's black community.

V. Black Loyalists and Sierra Leone

Events in England, France, and their remaining American colonies influenced events in the newly independent United States. When the defeated British forces evacuated New York in 1783, three thousand African Americans left with them. Many of these people settled in Nova Scotia, but others sailed for England. There, the black community, now freed by the *Somerset* decision, competed for jobs with white Britons. The British economy, stretched by the Seven Years War and weakened by the American Revolution, could not easily absorb these new workers. The result was a growing population of black poor in London and other urban centers.

The presence of free black poor people posed both a humanitarian and an ideological problem for British reformers or "abolitionists." These men and women wanted to abolish the slave trade. They used many of the same arguments as the nineteenth-century abolitionists, who wanted an immediate end to slavery in America, but this abolition movement was based in England. British abolitionists Granville Sharp and Thomas Clarkson, and black abolitionists Olaudah Equiano and Ottabah Cogoano, had been arguing against the slave trade, and joining in the call to emancipate the slaves of the West Indies. Defenders of slavery argued that the West Indian sugar economy demanded slave labor, and that African slaves were not suited by nature to be free workers. They pointed to the large population of unemployed black men in England as proof. The British abolitionists formed the Society for the Abolition of Slavery in 1787, and proposed an ingenious solution. England could make a stand against the slave trade by establishing a colony in West Africa. This colony would have economic as well as moral benefits, as it would open African markets for British goods, provide raw materials to England, create markets for African goods and reduce the appeal of the slave trade to those African nations which profited by selling their enemies to the Europeans. To people the colony, the British could send the black Americans now unemployed in England. These colonists, most of whom had adopted Christianity in America, would help evangelize the African continent. These divergent motives made the Sierra Leone colony similar to Britain's earlier colonial ventures in North America.

The Sierra Leone Company, under the advice of the antislavery philanthropists, hired Olaudah Equiano as quartermaster of the expedition. But after coming to see the conflicting motives among the various factions involved, and the mismanagement of the expedition by self-interested parties, Equiano withdrew his support, while a shipload of emigrants waited on the docks to embark for Sierra Leone. Nevertheless, three ships full of black migrants sailed for Africa in 1787, founding the city of Freetown and the colony of Sierra Leone.

The British philanthropists sent an emissary to America, William Thornton, a young doctor with antislavery convictions. Thornton proposed the Sierra Leone settlement to free African Americans. In New England, where he arrived first, he was warmly received, and black leaders Prince Hall and Paul Cuffee encouraged Thornton to find colonists in Philadelphia. But the Philadelphians, whatever lines of discrimination kept them out of the mainstream, preferred their community in Philadelphia to any prospective settlements in Sierra Leone. Thornton, for his part, remained in America, continuing to promote emigration by blacks to Africa. A doctor and opponent of slavery, Thornton is chiefly remembered for submitting a winning design in a contest to design a new Capitol for the United States—the elegant dome above the home of Congress was Thornton's idea.

VI. *France and* Haiti

The American Revolution had an impact on America's first ally, France. France, like England, was in serious economic trouble as a result of two costly (one disastrously so) wars. A series of bad harvests in the mid-1780s brought on a political crisis. In 1789 the crisis resulted in revolution, toppling the monarchy, the aristocracy, and the established church. To explain and justify these radical steps, France's Assembly adopted a Declaration of the Rights of Man, inspired by the American Declaration, and asserting the same self-evident truths to which the Americans had pledged their lives, fortunes, and sacred honor fourteen years earlier. Most Americans hailed the French Revolution as a continuation of their own.

In St. Domingue (now Haiti), France's most important colony, the French Revolution had profound implications. St. Domingue's wealth came from sugar plantations worked by black slaves. When the French Assembly invited colonies to send delegations to Paris, white planters, who controlled St. Domingue's economy, and free mulattos, who sought more power on the island, each sent representatives. Which delegation represented St. Domingue? On the island, the refusal of wealthy plantation owners and other whites to grant equal citizenship rights to the free people of color led to civil war. The slaves, under the leadership of Boukman and Toussaint L'Ouverture, rose up in rebellion. During ten years of bloody conflict, the slaves and their free black leaders defeated French, British, and Spanish armies sent to suppress their revolution.

When the United States and France became engaged in a quasi-war in 1798 (neither nation formally declared one), President John Adams opened negotiations with the black rebels on St. Domingue, led by Toussaint L'Ouverture, the brilliant self-educated son of slave parents. The United States supplied Toussaint's forces with weapons to fight their French former masters. When Napoleon took power in France, he sought to restore slavery and sugar production in St. Domingue, but the army he sent, led by his brother-in-law, was destroyed by Toussaint's superior generalship and decimated by yellow fever. Napoleon managed to capture Toussaint by trickery, and the general died in a French prison, but Napoleon could not suppress the spirit of liberty in Haiti. In 1804, it became the second independent republic in the New World.

Napoleon had held great dreams of recreating France's New World empire, beginning with the colony of Louisiana, which gave France control of the Mississippi.

But without St. Domingue, he could not develop Louisiana. Napoleon turned his attention to asserting control of the European continent. At this moment negotiators arrived in Paris from the United States, interested in securing for Americans the right to use the port of New Orleans. Napoleon offered to sell them all of Louisiana for $15 million.

VII. Expansion of Slavery

The Haitian Revolution and the Louisiana Purchase begin another story in American, and African American, history. While the founders of the American republic had not ended slavery throughout the new nation, they had barred slavery in American territories north of the Ohio River (1800) and ended the African slave trade (1807). Eight states had either ended slavery altogether, or had passed laws to eliminate the institution gradually, typically by freeing slaves born after a certain date. Maryland and Delaware, which did not abolish the institution, encouraged manumission, and some Virginia slave holders, including Edward Coles, James Madison's secretary, and John Randolph, Republican leader of the House of Representatives, settled their former slaves as free people on farms in Ohio and Illinois.

But the American acquisition of Louisiana, provoked by Napoleon's inability to defeat Toussaint, would have a tremendous impact on the future development of the United States. The Mississippi had formed a border for the United States. Spain controlled the Mississippi, along with the rivers flowing through Georgia, Alabama, and Mississippi into the Gulf of Mexico. With no outlets to the sea, the territory was worth little to American farmers—certainly it would not be worth the effort it would take to dislodge the Chicasaw, Choctaw, and Creek people who controlled the region. Spain, and British agents in Pensacola and Mobile, traded with these native peoples, keeping their friendship against any American encroachment. But when France sold Louisiana to the Americans, the power dynamic in the region shifted in favor of the United States.

Along with this political barrier, the Americans removed a technological barrier to development. The vast interior region stretching from the Appalachians in Georgia to the Mississippi River would become an ideal place to grow cotton, but until the 1790s cotton was not a profitable crop for Americans. It was grown on the Georgia and South Carolina sea islands, but it needed hours of intense labor to separate seeds from the bolls of cotton, and to comb the fibers to prepare for spinning. The state of Georgia, wanting to move settlement inland from the rice-producing seacoast, held a contest to design an invention to solve this problem. New Englander Eli Whitney, visiting the Georgia plantation of fellow New Englander Catherine Greene (her late husband, Nathanael Greene, former Quaker from Rhode Island, had been one of Washington's best generals), put his mind to this problem. Whitney's "cotton engine" cleaned the cotton bolls and aligned the fibers with the crank of a handle. While Whitney went on to mass-produce guns, his cotton gin made cotton the leading American export by 1820. The labor of planting and harvesting cotton, and then "ginning" the bolls through Whitney's machine, would be done by black men and women, as slavery would spread through the newly opened territories of Georgia, Alabama, and Mississippi.

First, though, the Native Americans had to be pushed from the region. In 1814, American forces under Andrew Jackson, supported by Choctaw warriors under Pushmataha, defeated the Creeks in Alabama. The previous year, William Henry Harrison had defeated a joint Native and British force led by the Shawnee leader Tecumseh and his brother Tenskwatwa ("The Prophet") at the Thames River, Ontario. This defeated the last resisting native people east of the Mississippi, and shortly afterward the United States developed the idea of moving its Indian allies, the Cherokees and Choctaws, west of the Mississippi. Spain still used its Gulf Coast outposts, Mobile and Pensacola, to encourage rebellion by slaves in Georgia, Alabama, and Mississippi, and to provide a refuge for runaway slaves. But in 1817 Andrew Jackson seized Pensacola, and Spain negotiated to sell Florida to the United States.

Sugar plantations had driven the slave trade in the eighteenth century. Now, in the nineteenth century, cotton plantations, with a similar insatiable demand for labor, would dominate the institution of slavery, and the political and economic institutions of the United States. Just as all regions of the colonies had participated in the eighteenth-century slave system, all would have a hand in the cotton economy. Cotton grown by enslaved African Americans in Georgia and Mississippi was converted into woven cloth in the factory mills of Massachusetts and Rhode Island. In 1787, it had seemed that slavery was bottled up, that it could expand no farther, and that liberty would vanquish slavery in America. But by 1817, the demand for slave labor was greater than ever. Since the African slave trade had been stopped in 1808, the increased demand for labor meant that now African Americans were moved from Virginia and South Carolina to the cotton plantations of Alabama and Mississippi or the sugar plantations of Louisiana. After the War of 1812, historian Henry Adams (great-grandson of John Adams) noted, Americans thought more about the price of cotton and less about the rights of man. But the fundamental principle Phillis Wheatley had called love of freedom remained in the hearts of the enslaved.

VIII. *Paul Cuffe and Denmark Vesey*

African Americans took different steps to act on their love of freedom. Paul Cuffe's father was an African brought to Massachusetts as a slave in the 1720s, and his mother was a Wampanoag Indian. A Quaker with close ties to the Rotch family (they had owned the ship which carried the East India Company's tea to Boston in 1773) Cuffe after the war had become one of the most successful African American businessmen of the day. He owned ships that traded between New England and the Chesapeake, and with Liverpool. His all-black crews caused a stir when they arrived in slave states or in the center of England's slave trade. Though the African American community of Philadelphia, led by Richard Allen, James Forten, and Absalom Jones, had rebuffed emissaries from London's Sierra Leone backers in the late 1780s, Cuffe was more receptive.

He believed that the Sierra Leone colony presented possibilities for an African American trading network. With resources of lumber and naval stores, Sierra Leone was closer to the lucrative South Atlantic whale hunting grounds. Cuffe envisioned using Sierra Leone as a base for his whaling interests. This would make the colony profitable, and could truly make it a refuge for displaced Africans. Cuffe sailed from Westport, Massachusetts, with nine families, eighteen adults and twenty children, in December 1815, to join the colony of Sierra Leone. Cuffe's own family remained in Massachusetts, where he returned six months later. Cuffe's aim was to build in the Sierra Leone colony an African economic trading base. But with the colony under the control of London, it was impossible for an American merchant like Cuffe to prosper in it. And as long as West Indian sugar plantations needed slaves, the slave trade would disrupt the economies and societies of West Africa.

Cuffe's death in 1817 ended the possibility of a viable commercial link between Africa and African Americans. Just as he was hoping to link together the various strands of the British antislavery movement, others in America were pursuing colonization as a solution to the problem of race and slavery in America. The American Colonization Society, founded in 1816, had as its goal the gradual emancipation of American slaves and their colonization to some place either in the Louisiana territory, or beyond the territorial limits of the United States. The Sierra Leone enterprise had begun with the motive of finding a safe haven for former slaves; the American Colonization Society's motive became the removal of free blacks from the United States. The white leaders of the A.C.S., including James Madison, Henry Clay, and John Marshall, had a genuine hatred for the institution of slavery. But they also believed that black and white Americans could not live together peacefully, that, whatever their own personal feelings, the majority of whites would not regard blacks as their equals, and that black men and women would be relegated to permanent second-class status. These leaders also feared that black men and women, having been enslaved for so long by whites, would never trust whites to treat them fairly. The A.C.S. launched the colony of Liberia in 1821 but found it very difficult to convince free blacks to emigrate. By the 1820s black Americans, slave and free, were no longer Africans. Home and family were in America, not in Africa, and their future lay in America.

But what kind of a future would it be? Would it be the kind of future Paul Cuffe envisioned, of free black men and women entering into trade with the wider world, as Americans? Or would it be a future constrained by the people who claimed ownership over black Americans? Denmark Vesey, a free black carpenter married to a slave woman, provided one answer in 1822. Vesey was an active member of Charleston's African Methodist Episcopal Church. He organized over a thousand South Carolina slaves in an attempt to seize their freedom by burning the city and killing its white inhabitants. June 16, 1822 was set as the day, but word leaked out. Vesey and other leaders were hanged; other participants were sold to the West Indies. A few escaped. There is evidence that David Walker, a tailor, was among them. Walker opened a tailor shop in Boston, and in 1829 wrote his *Appeal to the Colored Citizens of the World*, urging enslaved people to act on their right to freedom, given by God and recognized by the hypocritical Americans in their Declaration of Independence. Enslaved people had the right to kill their enslavers, Walker said, and he sent copies of his pamphlet in barrels of clothing made in New England for the plantation slaves of the South.

IX. Slavery and National Politics

Slavery became a national political issue in 1820, when the Missouri territory applied for statehood. Noting that most of Missouri lay north of the Ohio River, where the Northwest Ordinance prohibited slavery, Congressman James Tallmadge of New York proposed that slavery be banned in Missouri. The Missouri debate touched a raw nerve in American politics, and brought up the specter of disunion. The real issue was the future of the American republic. Ultimately Congress resolved the question through an elaborate compromise: Missouri was admitted to the Union as a slave state; Maine, until then part of Massachusetts, was admitted to the Union as a free state; and slavery would be prohibited north of the 36 degrees and 30 minutes line (Missouri's southern border). This line made most of the Louisiana territory free, and seemed at least temporarily to have halted slavery's spread.

But the Missouri debate had touched off something else. In Congress, little of the Missouri debate hinged on the morality of slavery; most of it dealt with Constitutional questions or the efficacy of slave versus free labor. Much of the attack on the institution of slavery warned that slavery weakened society, or that a black population posed dangers in white society. This racist element was new, and made this debate very different from earlier discussions of slavery.

In Congress, Charles Pinckney of South Carolina defended the right of slaveholders to bring their property into Missouri, and grew quite elegiac when he recounted how blacks and whites had fought together to secure American independence. James Madison noted that although Massachusetts congressmen led the effort to keep slavery out of Missouri, their own state prohibited blacks from serving in the militia or serving on juries. Thomas Jefferson, who half a century earlier had tried to condemn England's king for piratical warfare against human nature, now blamed England for stirring up the Missouri trouble. Abolition, Jefferson said, was an English hobbyhorse, one they would ride to death, not in the interest of freeing slaves, but merely to cause trouble for American republicans.

X. Spirit of Liberty

The spirit of liberty, which Phillis Wheatley saw as implanted in every human breast, had brought the American republic into being. Phillis Wheatley could with no apparent contradiction condemn slavery and write a poem celebrating George Washington, who received her poem as a signal honor. The American Revolution had awakened the spirit of liberty everywhere, but by 1820 the American republic had confined to white men alone the enjoyment of liberty. While half of the American states had prohibited slavery by 1820, there were by that year more slaves in America than there had been Americans in 1775, and more than a million American slaves would be sold from Virginia and the Carolinas to Alabama, Mississippi, Louisiana, and Missouri by 1860.

Though the spirit of liberty would be constrained and confined, it could not be extinguished. The American Revolution had awakened it, and it would continue to glow in the hearts of the oppressed, as Phillis Wheatley had written it would. It would stir the nation again, when revived in the hearts of Frederick Douglass and Harriet Tubman, Abraham Lincoln and William Lloyd Garrison, Fannie Lou Hamer and Martin Luther King, Jr.

LESSON 1

Human Liberation Versus the State

The Africans who arrived in Virginia aboard a "Dutch Man of Warr" in 1619 provide the earliest record of a black presence in the British colonies. They were incorporated into the colonial labor force as indentured servants and provided the nucleus for what became the free black community in colonial America.

Other Africans arrived in Virginia and Maryland after 1619. Before 1661 there were slaves, indentured servants, and free blacks within the populations of the colonies, but by the beginning of the eighteenth century, indentured servitude was no longer an option for Africans in America. By the close of the century, two communities of African Americans emerged from the colonial experience. One group was enslaved permanently, whereas, tacitly, the other was comprised of "free persons." From the beginning of the eighteenth century until the end of the Civil War, the legal status for most black people in America was that of slave.

By 1770, three main population groups were apparent in British North America: Native Americans, European Americans and African Americans. Whites grouped African Americans as blacks—enslaved or free—largely ignorant or uncaring of the fact that they came from various tribes and continental African empires. On the eve of the American Revolution and beyond, all three groups searched in different ways for an American identity. The European Americans could look for it within the meaning of their British colonial experience. The Native Americans and the African Americans would, without leaving their ethnic identities behind, search for their place within English common law and, later, under the U.S. Constitution.

Organizing Idea

African Americans used the British colonial courts and later U.S. courts to achieve emancipation from slavery. Their assertions formed a tradition of legal protest and became a "weapon of choice" for black persons, both slave and free, who wished to attack the legal foundations of slavery (constitutions, statutes, and usage) and the legacy of slavery (racism, discrimination, and inequality).

Student Objectives

Students will:

- compare and discuss the Second Charter of Virginia and the First Charter of Massachusetts, discerning and discussing "the rights of Englishmen"
- become familiar with key documents from the Revolutionary Period, which defined the rights of citizens of the new nation and those held in bondage
- understand how American independence from British colonial "slavery" created expectations for expanded rights among marginalized and objectified people and groups such as landless whites, women, and Native Americans in the thirteen colonies (Nowhere was this expectation more deeply felt and more eloquently expressed than among African Americans.)

Key Questions

- Can a contract give a person property rights in another person, such as he might have in an animal, an article of clothing, or an automobile?
- Can human law deprive a person of natural rights?
- What are natural rights, and how does humankind get them?
- What are the elements of the British law (The Magna Carta, the Common Law, the English Bill of Rights, the Habeas Corpus Act, the Petition of Right, and custom and tradition), and why are they important to our conception of liberty?
- Who was a slave in America?
- How did the U.S. Constitution settle the question of slavery?

Primary Source Materials

DOCUMENT 2.1.1: Excerpt from the "Introduction to the Laws and Customs of England" by Henry de Bracton, an English Judge of the Court (known as King's Bench) in Thirteenth-Century England

DOCUMENT 2.1.2: Excerpts from the Second Charter of Virginia, May 24, 1609

DOCUMENT 2.1.3: Excerpts from the First Charter of Massachusetts, March 4, 1629

DOCUMENT 2.1.4: Slave Petition to the Massachusetts Legislature, 1773

DOCUMENT 2.1.5: Excerpts from Slave Petition to Governor Gage, 1774

DOCUMENT 2.1.6A AND B: Image and transcription of 1777 petition presented to the Massachusetts Legislature by Prince Hall and eight other black Bostonians

DOCUMENT 2.1.7A AND B: Image and transcription of the original draft of the Declaration of Independence, 1776

DOCUMENT 2.1.8: Articles I, X, and XI of the Massachusetts Bill of Rights, 1780

Supplementary Materials

ITEM 2.1.A: Additional vocabulary lists for primary sources

ITEM 2.1.B: Excerpt from "A Sketch of the Laws Relating to Slavery in the Several States of the United States of America, A Northern Perspective," by George M. Stroud, 1856.

ITEM 2.1.C: Excerpt from "An Historical Sketch of Slavery, A Southern Perspective from Law of Freedom and Bondage: Inquiry into the Law of Negro Slavery in the USA," by Thomas R. R. Cobb

Note: These excerpts from histories of the slave trade were written many years after the time period of this lesson. As such, they are secondary sources. However, because they offer perspectives on the ways historians of the mid-1800s viewed the slave trade, they also serve as primary sources for that time.

Vocabulary

bicameral parliament	iniquitous	*partus se quitur patrem*	ratification
caste	investiture		royal charter
dichotomy	law of nature	*partus se quitur ventrem*	statute
inalienable	natural rights	protocol	

Student Activities

Activity 1 — **Reading and Discussion—The Rights of a British Subject**

One of the great challenges in teaching the colonial era is overcoming the disconnection that textbooks impose. The "we" (Yankees)—"they" (British) dichotomy promoted in most textbooks is pervasive and suggests that colonists did not consider themselves as British. The instructional task is to awaken in students an awareness that Great Britain was the "superpower" of that day, "number one" in military might both on land and sea. The governance was orderly and understood; the King was head of state and the Prime Minister was head of government. The colonies were ruled by a bicameral parliament, one part elected, one inherited. There was no written constitution, but England was nevertheless a nation of laws and customs. The British empire was global in scope, and the colonists were proud to be British. It was only after the Seven Years War (French and Indian) that the fraying of the "mystic chords of union" began.

- Explain the role of Great Britain in the Atlantic World in the eighteenth century and then read aloud the "Introduction to the Laws and Customs of England" (2.1.1). Have students imagine and describe how it may have felt to be a citizen of Great Britain.

- Ask students to describe in writing how unwritten laws and customs might protect "the rights of Englishmen." Interested student should read the entire summary online.
- Have students read the excerpts from the colonial charters from Massachusetts and Virginia (2.1.2 and 2.1.3) and discuss the rights of Englishmen in the colonies.

Reading and Analysis—Paths to Freedom

Activity 2

Have students work in small groups, with each group responsible for one document, to read and analyze Documents 2.1.4–2.1.7, reporting back to the class as a whole. What do the petitions tell you about slaves' expectations regarding their rights? Students analyzing the petitions should compare findings. How do the documents differ? What changes, if any, are there between the petitions submitted before and after the Declaration of Independence? How do these documents relate to Documents 2.1.2–2.1.3?

Note: In each instance, the legislature failed to act on the petition.

Comparing and Contrasting—Rights in a New Nation

Activity 3

Both the original and a transcription of the draft of the Declaration of Independence are available on the CD-ROM (2.1.7a and 2.1.7b). Teachers can select whichever is appropriate for students, but all students will be interested to see the marked-up text even if they work with the typed version. Read the draft aloud as well as the relevant articles from the Massachusetts Bill of Rights (2.1.8). How do the rights granted in these documents differ from those in the colonial charters? Look at the Declaration of Independence that was enacted. How does it differ from the draft version? Why might this be?

Discussion—Who Is a Slave?

Activity 4

Distribute the essays by Thomas R. R. Cobb and George M. Stroud (Items 2.1.B and 2.1.C) and have students define the terms *partus sequitur patrem* and *partus sequitur ventrem*. In the common law how did these terms apply? To whom did they not apply? Have students discuss how applying these laws to black people dehumanized them and institutionalized slavery. The essays are likely to evoke strong reactions, and students may wish to respond by writing a letter to the authors.

Further Student and Teacher Resources

Collier, Christopher, and James Collier. *The Paradox of Jamestown, 1585–1700.* New York: Benchmark Books, 1998. (juvenile literature)

> **Music Connection**
>
> ✣
>
> Enslaved men and women sang "hollers" or "calls" as they worked. A song like "Arwhoolie"—a cornfield holler (available on the CD-ROM)—would be sung by a lone person, without accompaniment. Sometimes they were used to send a message across the fields to the house or to others working nearby. More often, men and women sang to ease their minds and to make the time pass faster so that the sun might set sooner and end the workday. These worksongs tended to be melancholy and led to the creation of blues songs. To experience the idea of a holler, ask the students to stand outside at a distance from each other and then to send a message by singing or by shouting it. Which can be better heard? Ask students if they hear any connection to the type of music practiced by heavy metal singers?

Earle, Alice Morse. *Home Life in Colonial Days*. Middle Village, NY: Jonathan David Publishers, 1975.

Haskins, James. *Building a New Land: African Americans in Colonial America*. New York: Harper Collins Publishers, 2001. (juvenile literature)

Saari, Peggy. *Colonial America, Primary Sources*. U.X.L. Colonial America Reference Library, The Gale Group, Farmington Hills, MI: 2000.

Schmittroth, Linda. *American Revolution, Primary Sources*. U.X.L. American Revolution Reference Library, The Gale Group, Farmington Hills, MI: 2000.

Schneider, Dorothy. *Slavery in America: From Colonial Times to the Civil War*. New York, Facts on File, 2000.

Van Sertima, Ivan. *They Came Before Columbus*. New York: Random House, 1976.

Video

Africans in America. Boston: WGBH Educational Foundation. PBS Video [distributor], 1998. A four-part video series chronicling the African American experience from 1450–1865.

> **Contemporary Connection**
>
> ✣
>
> **For Historical Research**
>
> Beginning in the late eighteenth century, a few enslaved African Americans took their owners to court to argue for their freedom. In 2003, an online archive of such lawsuits filed in St Louis, Missouri, became accessible to the public. (The Old Courthouse in St. Louis was the setting for the Dred Scott case in 1846. See Sourcebook 3, Lesson 15.) The St. Louis Circuit Court Historical Records Project contains more than 280 legal documents filed between 1814 and 1860, as well as images of original handwritten documents by black men, women, and children who used the court systems to seek freedom. For more information and to view these archives, visit *http://stlcourtrecords.wustl.edu*. Students should research court records in their state to see whether any petitions for freedom were filed before Emancipation.

Primary Source Material for Lesson 1

2.1.1

Excerpt from the "Introduction to the Laws and Customs of England" by Henry de Bracton, an English Judge of the Court (known as King's Bench) in Thirteenth-Century England

[England alone uses within her boundaries unwritten law and custom]
 Though in almost all lands use is made of the *leges* [laws] and the *jus scriptum* [laws written], England alone uses unwritten law and custom. There law derives from nothing written [but] from what usage has approved. Nevertheless, it will not be absurd to call English laws leges [laws], though they are unwritten, since whatever has been rightly decided and approved with the counsel and consent of the magnates and the general agreement of the *res publica* [the republic], the authority of the king or prince having first been added thereto, has the force of law. England has as well many local customs, varying from place to place, for the English have many things by custom which they do not have by law, as in the various counties, cities, boroughs and villages, where it will always be necessary to learn what the custom of the place is and how those who allege it use it.

The full text of Document 2.1.1 is available on the CD-ROM.

2.1.2

Excerpts from the Second Charter of Virginia, May 24, 1609

AND we do further . . . ORDAIN and establish, that the said Treasurer and Council here resident, and their Successors, or any four of them, being assembled (the Treasurer being one) shall, from time to time, have full Power and Authority to admit and receive any other Person into their Company, Corporation, and Freedom; And further, in a General Assembly of the Adventurers with the consent of the greater Part, upon Good Cause, to disfranchise and put out any Person or Persons, out of the said Freedom or Company . . . ALSO, we do . . . DECLARE . . . that all and every Persons being our Subjects, which shall go and inhabit within the said Colony and Plantation, and every their Children and Posterity; which shall happen to be born within any Limits thereof, shall HAVE and ENJOY all Liberties, Franchises, and Immunities of Free Denizens and natural Subjects within any of our other Dominions to all Interests and Purposes, as if they had been abiding and born within this our realm of England . . .

The full text of Document 2.1.2 is available on the CD-ROM.

2.1.3

Excerpts from the First Charter of Massachusetts, March 4, 1629

And . . . wee doe graunte to the saide Governor and Company . . . That all and every the Subjects of V's . . . which shall . . . inhabite within the saide Landes . . . , shall have and enjoy all liberties and Immunities of free and naturall Subjects within any of the Domynions of V's . . . And . . . it shall and maie be lawful to and for the Governor for the Tyme being as shalbe assembled in any of their generall Courts to be specially summoned and assembled for that Purpose or the greater maie wynn and incite the Natives of Country, to the Knowledge and Obedience of the onlie true God and Sauior of Mankinde, and the Christian Fayth, which in our Royall Intencon, and the Adventurers free Profession, is the principall Ende of this Plantation . . .

The full text of Document 2.1.3 is available on the CD-ROM.

2.1.4

Slave Petition to the Massachusetts Legislature, 1773

Sir,

The efforts made by the legislative of this province in their last sessions to free themselves from slavery, gave us, who are in that deplorable state, a high degree of satisfaction. We expect great things from men who have made such a noble stand against the designs of their fellow-men to enslave them. We cannot but wish and hope, Sir, that you will have the same grand object, we mean civil and religious liberty, in view of your next session. The divine spirit of freedom, seems to fire every humane breast on this continent, except such as are bribed to assist in executing the execrable pain . . . .

We do not pretend to dictate to you Sir, or to the honorable Assembly, of which you are a member: we acknowledge our obligations to you for what you have done already, but as the people of this province seem to be actuated by the principles of equity and justice, we cannot but expect your house will again take our deplorable case into serious consideration, and give us that ample relief which, as men, we have a natural right to . . . .

The full text of Document 2.1.4 is available on the CD-ROM.

2.1.5

Excerpts from Slave Petition to Governor Gage, 1774

Your Petitioners apprehind we have in common with all other men and naturel right to our freedoms without Being depriv'd of them by our fellow men as we are freeborn Pepel and have never forfeited this Blessing by aney compact or agreement whatever. But we were unjustly dragged by the cruel hand of power from our dearest frinds and sum of us stolen from the bosoms of our tender Parents and from a Populous Pleasant and plentiful country and Brought hither to be made slaves for Life in a Christian land. Thus we are deprived of every thing that hath a tendency to make life even tolerable, the endearing ties of husband and wife we are strangers to . . . Our children are also taken from us by force and sent maney miles from us . . . Thus our Lives are imbittered . . . there is a great number of us sencear . . . members of the Church of Christ how can the master and the slave be said to fulfil that command Live in love let Brotherly love contuner and abound Beare my Borden when he Beares me down with the . . . Chanes of slavery . . . Nither can we reap an equal benefit from the laws of the Land which doth not justifi but condemns Slavery or if there had bin aney Law to hold us in Bondage . . . there never was aney to enslave our children for life when Born in a Free Countrey. We therefore Bage your Excellency and Honours will . . . cause an act of legislative to be passed that we may obtain our natural right our freedoms and our children to be set a lebety at the year of twenty-one.

2.1.6A AND B

Image and transcription of 1777 petition presented to the Massachusetts Legislature by Prince Hall and eight other black Bostonians

(In imitat)ion of the Lawdable Example of the Good People of these States your petitioners have Long and Patiently waited the Event of petition after petition. By them presented to the Legislative Body of this state and cannot but with Grief Reflect that their Success hath been but too similar they Cannot but express their Astonishment that It have Never Bin Considered that Every Principle from which America has Acted in the Course of their unhappy Difficulties with Great Briton Pleads Stronger than A thousand arguments in favors of your petitioners they therfor humble Beseech your honours to give this petition its due weight and consideration & cause an act of the legislature to be past Wherby they may be Restored to the Enjoyments of that which is the Natural right of all men—and their Children who wher Born in this Land of Liberty may not be held as Slaves after they arrive at the age of twenty one years so may the Inhabitance of this States No longer chargeable with the inconstancy of acting themselves that part which they condemn and oppose in others Be prospered in their present Glorious struggle for Liberty and have those Blessings to them, &c.

The full text of Document 2.1.6b is available on the CD-ROM.

2.1.7A AND B

Image and transcription of the original draft of the Declaration of Independence, 1776

he has waged cruel war against human nature itself, violating its most sacred rights of life & liberty in the persons of a distant people who never offended him, captivating & carrying them into slavery in another hemisphere, or to incur miserable death in their transportation thither. this piratical warfare, the opprobrium of infidel powers, is the warfare of the CHRISTIAN king of Great Britain. determined to keep open a market where MEN should be bought & sold, he has prostituted his negative for suppressing every legislative attempt to prohibit or to restrain this execrable commerce: and that this assemblage of horrors might want no fact of distinguished die, he is now exciting those very people to rise in arms among us, and to purchase that liberty of which he has deprived them, & murdering the people upon whom he also obtruded them; thus paying off former crimes committed against the liberties of one people, with crimes which he urges them to commit against the lives of another.

The full text of Document 2.1.7b is available on the CD-ROM.

2.1.6A
1777 Petition

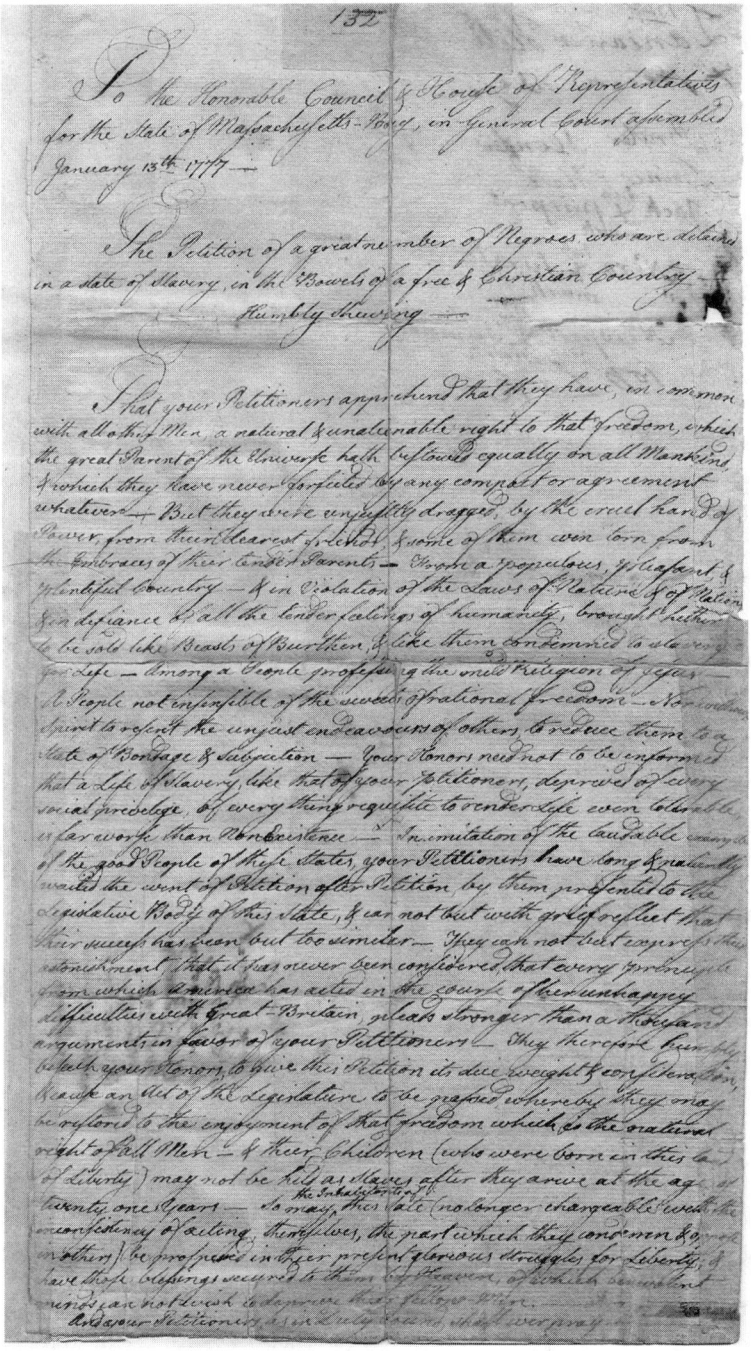

To the Honorable Council & House of Representatives for the State of Massachusetts-Bay, in General Court assembled January 13th 1777—

The Petition of a great number of Negroes who are detained in a state of Slavery, in the Bowels of a free & Christian Country—
Humbly shewing

That your Petitioners apprehend that they have, in common with all other Men, a natural & unalienable right to that freedom, which the great Parent of the Universe hath bestowed equally on all Mankind & which they have never forfeited by any compact or agreement whatever—But they were unjustly dragged, by the cruel hand of Power, from their dearest friends & some of them even torn from the Embraces of their tender Parents—From a populous, pleasant & plentiful country—& in violation of the Laws of Nature & of Nations & in defiance of all the tender feelings of humanity, brought hither to be sold like Beasts of Burthen, & like them condemned to Slavery for Life—Among a People professing the mild Religion of Jesus. A People not insensible of the sweets of rational freedom—Nor without Spirit to resent the unjust endeavours of others to reduce them to a State of Bondage & Subjection—Your Honors need not to be informed that a Life of Slavery, like that of your Petitioners, deprived of every social privelege, of every thing requisite to render Life even tolerable, is far worse than Nonexistence—In imitation of the laudable example of the good People of these States, your Petitioners have long & patiently waited the event of Petition after Petition by them presented to the Legislative Body of this State, & cannot but with grief reflect that their success has been but too similar—They can not but express their astonishment that it has never been considered that every principle from which America has acted in the course of their unhappy difficulties with Great-Britain, pleads stronger than a thousand arguments in favor of your Petitioners—They therefore humbly beseech your Honors, to give this Petition its due weight & consideration & cause an Act of the Legislature to be passed whereby they may be restored to the enjoyment of that freedom which is the natural right of all Men—& their Children (who were born in this Land of Liberty) may not be held as Slaves after they arrive at the age of twenty one Years—So may the Inhabitants of this State (no longer chargeable with the inconsistency of acting, themselves, the part which they condemn & oppose in others) be prospered in their present glorious struggles for Liberty, & have those blessings secured to them by Heaven, of which benevolent minds can not wish to deprive their fellow Men.
And your Petitioners as in Duty bound shall ever pray.

Courtesy of Massachusetts Archives

2.1.7A
Original draft of the Declaration of Independence

A Declaration by the Representatives of the UNITED STATES OF AMERICA, in General Congress assembled.

When in the course of human events it becomes necessary for one people to dissolve the political bands which have connected them with another, and to assume among the powers of the earth the separate and equal station to which the laws of nature & of nature's god entitle them, a decent respect to the opinions of mankind requires that they should declare the causes which impel them to the separation.

We hold these truths to be self-evident, that all men are created equal, that they are endowed by their creator with equal rights inherent & inalienable, among which are the preservation of life, & liberty, & the pursuit of happiness; that to secure these ends, governments are instituted among men, deriving their just powers from the consent of the governed; that whenever any form of government becomes destructive of these ends, it is the right of the people to alter or to abolish it, & to institute new government, laying it's foundation on such principles & organising it's powers in such form, as to them shall seem most likely to effect their safety & happiness. prudence indeed will dictate that governments long established should not be changed for light & transient causes: and accordingly all experience hath shewn that mankind are more disposed to suffer while evils are sufferable, than to right themselves by abolishing the forms to which they are accustomed. but when a long train of abuses & usurpations [begun at a distinguished period & pursuing invariably the same object, evinces a design to reduce them under absolute despotism,] it is their right, it is their duty, to throw off such government, & to provide new guards for their future security. such has been the patient sufferance of these colonies; & such is now the necessity which constrains them to expunge their former systems of government. the history of the present king of Great Britain is a history of unremitting injuries and usurpations, among which appears no solitary fact to contradict the uniform tenor of the rest [all of which have] in direct object the establishment of an absolute tyranny over these states. to prove this let facts be submitted to a candid world, for the truth of which we pledge a faith yet unsullied by falsehood.

Courtesy of the Library of Congress

2.1.8

Articles I, X, and XI of the Massachusetts Bill of Rights, 1780

Art. I.—All men are born free and equal, and have certain natural, essential, and unalienable rights; among which may be reckoned the right of enjoying and defending their lives and liberties; that of acquiring, possessing, and protecting property; in fine, that of seeking and obtaining their safety and happiness.

The full text of Document 2.1.8 is available on the CD-ROM.

LESSON 2

African Americans in the American Revolution

Although excluded from serving in the Massachusetts and Connecticut colonial militias by laws passed in the mid-seventeenth century, free black men had volunteered and been accepted to help fight in the early skirmishes against the Indians and the French in British colonial America. An estimated five thousand black men fought on the British side in the Seven Year (French and Indian) War. Whatever their intention, the effect of these laws was to deny these black warriors status as *regulars*, soldiers recognized as legitimate combatants in war, who were entitled to a soldier's pay and benefits. Prior to the Revolution, the military service of free black men in colonial conflicts, if historically valiant, was officially gratuitous. It merited no official recognition.

The question of whether black slaves should serve as soldiers, however, was an issue that raised fears and questions for both the white and the slave communities. For the white colonists, there were fears of assassination, of armed rebellion, and of black people providing aid and comfort to their enemies in time of war. By the time of the American Revolution, their own personal freedom, equality, and security were very real concerns for black slaves throughout the thirteen colonies. Could white colonists be trusted to provide and protect black freedom following the Revolution? Would masters have to be compensated for emancipated soldiers? Would black soldiers receive the bonuses, land, and pensions promised to white soldiers? How could white colonists be sure that emancipated black veterans would be able to support themselves and their families, and not be thrown upon the mercy of the local community? Would black veterans be allowed to coexist with white people on terms of equality after the war?

Those slaves who had the option to choose whether or not to serve as soldiers chose the side that offered them the best prospect of freedom. While the colonists debated, denied, and deferred official soldier status to slaves, the British recognized the colonials' dilemma and moved quickly to secure the services of slaves as soldiers, sailors, and spies. Lord Dunmore's Proclamation, offering slaves freedom for fighting on the British side, compelled the colonists, especially in the South, to compete for the loyalty and services of their slave populations and to arm them. Two colonies, South Carolina and Georgia, refused.

In exchange for their loyalty, the British evacuated three thousand black men, women, and children when the war ended. This prevented reenslavement by their owners after the Treaty of Paris was ratified. Many thousands more slaves were abandoned, however, and left to the mercy of owners returning to claim their property, including the slaves who had escaped or been taken during the war. Some of the slaves who were sympathetic to the British fled to the frontier or to Native American communities to escape the vengeance of their masters and of the nation they had chosen not to serve.

The number of black slave-soldiers who were set free by the colonies and states following the Revolutionary War cannot be accounted with certainty. Some, like George Washington's slave, William Lee, would be free only upon the death of their masters, provided, of course, they survived them. The feats and fates of some of those that chose to serve the cause of American freedom can be best learned from the documents they themselves bequeathed us. This lesson is the first of two to examine African American participation in the Revolutionary War. The second (Lesson 3) will look at those who sided with the British.

Organizing Idea

The question of whether to allow free and enslaved African Americans to fight posed a complex dilemma for the colonists. In time, free and enslaved African Americans from all but two colonies fought alongside white soldiers in the Revolutionary War and were a crucial factor in the war effort.

Student Objectives

Students will:

- understand the important role of African Americans in the American Revolution
- analyze the actions and decisions around the issue of African Americans in the military
- explore why information often is left out of history books

Key Questions

- What was the policy of the thirteen colonies on African Americans in the military?
- Why would African Americans choose to fight?
- What were the roles of African Americans in the Revolutionary War?
- Why have African Americans been left out of the story of the American Revolution?

Primary Source Materials

DOCUMENT 2.2.1: Resolution passed by the Massachusetts Committee of Safety, May 1775

DOCUMENT 2.2.2: Council of War proposal, October 8, 1775

DOCUMENT 2.2.3: Letter from George Washington to Nicholas Cooke, January 2, 1778

DOCUMENT 2.2.4: Response by Massachusetts legislature to a petition for a colored regiment, 1778

DOCUMENT 2.2.5: Letter from Alexander Hamilton to John Jay, President of Congress, March 14, 1779

DOCUMENT 2.2.6: Excerpts from letters exchanged between George Washington and Henry Laurens, March 1779

DOCUMENT 2.2.7: Excerpts from a Congressional Committee resolution, March 29, 1779

DOCUMENTS 2.2.8: Excerpts from an act of the Rhode Island legislature, February 1778

DOCUMENT 2.2.9: Image of "Hope," the First Rhode Island Continental Regiment flag

DOCUMENT 2.2.10: Excerpt from a speech by Governor Eustis of Massachusetts on the First Rhode Island Regiment, December 12, 1820

DOCUMENT 2.2.11: Excerpts from an address delivered in 1842 before the Congregational and Presbyterian Anti-Slavery Society at Francestown, New Hampshire, by Dr. Harris, a Revolutionary War veteran and member of the First Rhode Island Regiment

DOCUMENT 2.2.12: Image of the Marquis de Lafayette at Yorktown, attended by James Armistead Lafayette

DOCUMENT 2.2.13: Image of James Armistead Lafayette and testimonial by the Marquis de Lafayette

DOCUMENT 2.2.14: Eulogy of James Forten, delivered by Robert Purvis, March 30, 1842

DOCUMENT 2.2.15: Excerpt from *The Colored Patriots of the American Revolution: With Sketches of Several Distinguished Colored Persons: To Which Is Added a Brief Survey of the Condition And Prospects of Colored Americans* by William Cooper Nell, 1855

DOCUMENT 2.2.16: Image of Oliver Cromwell's discharge signed by George Washington

DOCUMENT 2.2.17: Letters by Charles Sedgewick and Agrippa Hull to Acting Secretary of State Richard Rush, June 12, 1828

DOCUMENT 2.2.18: Petition on behalf of Salem Poor, December 1775

DOCUMENT 2.2.19: Excerpt from "Sketches of Bunker Hill Battle," by Samuel Swett, 1818 from William Cooper Nell's *The Colored Patriots of the American Revolution*, 1855

DOCUMENT 2.2.20: Image of Peter Salem at Bunker Hill, from William Cooper Nell's *The Colored Patriots of the American Revolution*, 1855

DOCUMENT 2.2.21: Drawing by Henry Pelham of Crispus Attucks in the Boston Massacre, 1770

DOCUMENT 2.2.22: Engraving by Paul Revere of Boston Massacre, 1770

Supplementary Materials

ITEM 2.2.A: Additional vocabulary lists for primary sources

Vocabulary

battalion	mulatto	regiment
discharge	recruit	traitor

Student Activities

Discussion: "Mainstream Myths"

Activity 1

Ask your students to recall some of the myths related to American history, for example, the story that George Washington threw a silver dollar across the Potomac River. Plumb the credibility (and incredibility) of these myths by introducing factors such as the shortage of coins and the value of money in the colonies. Ask your students to speculate how these myths entered American history as privileged stories—stories that are told and retold as true. How do we know what is "history" and what's not? How can you tell truth from myth?

Creating a Time Line—Enlistment of African Americans

Activity 2

Using Documents 2.2.1–2.2.7 have students read over the information. Then on a time line of 1775–1785, have students plot the event or decision and have them determine what it meant for African Americans in the military. When did the position on African Americans in the military seem to change categorically? Why did it change?

60 Minutes Activity

Activity 3

The purpose of this activity is to have groups of students synthesize and present information they have read to the rest of the class in an interesting and informative way. It involves many primary sources; however, each group of students will only examine a few. The class is going to create a *60 Minutes*–style news and information program; the focus of the program is African Americans in the Revolutionary War. The goal for each group is to introduce the rest of the class to a person or group from the Revolutionary War. Each group receives a packet of information. The packets contain two elements: background and context information and related primary sources. After reading over the materials, each group plans a presentation.

The presentation should be about five minutes maximum in length.

Feel free to create your own structure or adapt the following to accommodate the needs of the groups. Each participant in the group needs to take an active role. People's roles could include: man/woman/group being interviewed, anchor/interviewer, an "audience" member with questions, or a person associated with the group/person at hand.

Suggestions for presentations:

- Interview the person/group they've read about.
- Have the group present a "this is your life" story for the person/group they read about.
- Have "audience members" ask questions of the guest(s).
- Re-create an important day/event in this person/group's life.
- Feel free to have students come up with their own news story format.

Personalities for groups:

First Rhode Island Regiment (2.2.8–2.2.11)

James Armistead Lafayette (2.2.12 and 2.2.13)

James Forten (2.2.14)

Oliver Cromwell (2.2.15 and 2.2.16)

Agrippa Hull (2.2.17)

Salem Poor and Peter Salem (2.2.18–2.2.20)

Activity 4 — Comparing and Contrasting Representations of the American Revolution

Have students examine the two images of the Boston Massacre (2.2.21 and 2.2.22). Ask them to compare and contrast the two paintings of the same event, created two weeks apart. What's similar? What's different?

Read the students some information about Crispus Attucks and the Boston massacre. How does it change the meaning or implication of the painting to have Attucks in the painting versus left out? Why might Paul Revere have left Crispus Attucks out of his painting? What might we learn from examining these two paintings?

Activity 5 — Reflection on the Involvement of African Americans in the Revolution

In his introduction to his book *Colored Patriots of the Revolution,* William Cooper Nell, the first published African American historian, wrote, "It is to be hoped that the reading of these sketches will give new self-respect and confidence to the race here represented. Let them emulate the noble deeds and sentiments of their ancestors, and feel that the dark skin can never be a badge of disgrace, while it has been ennobled by such examples." Summarize the lessons with a final discussion. Ask students to respond to Nell's words. What new information have they learned? What would they like to learn more about and how could they find that information? Why have African Americans been left out of the story of the American Revolution? Teachers are also encouraged to return to the key questions and incorporate them into this final, summarizing discussion.

Further Student and Teacher Resources

Buckley, Gail. *American Patriots: The Story of Blacks in the Military from the Revolution to Desert Storm.* New York: Random House, 2001.

———. (Adapted for young people by Tonya Bolden.) *American Patriots: The Story of Blacks in the Military from the Revolution to Desert Storm.* New York: Crown Publishers, 2003.

Garrison, William Lloyd. *The Loyalty and Devotion of Colored Americans in the Revolution and the War of 1812.* Boston: R. F. Wallcut, 1861.

Kaplan, Sidney and Emma Nogrady Kaplan. *The Black Presence in the Era of the American Revolution.* Amherst, MA: The University of Massachusetts Press, 1989.

Quarles, Benjamin. *The Negro in the American Revolution.* Chapel Hill: University of North Carolina Press, 1961.

Quintal, George, Jr. *Patriots of Color 'A Peculiar Beauty and Merit'—African Americans and Native Americans at Battle Road & Bunker Hill,* Boston and Minute Man National Historic Parks, February 2002.

Wilkes. Laura E. *Missing Pages in American History, Revealing the Services of Negroes in the Early Wars in the United States of America 1641–1815.* Washington, D.C.: Press of R. L. Pendleton, 1919.

Wilson, Joseph T. *The Black Phalanx: A History of the Negro Soldier of the United States in the War of 1775–1812, 1861–1865.* Hartford, CT: American Publishing Co., 1888.

Websites

www.americanrevolution.org

http://docsouth.unc.edu

www.pbs.org/wgbh/aia/

www.loc.gov

Contemporary Connection

✴

A Little-Known History

The Black Revolutionary War Patriots Foundation is currently planning a memorial, built on the National Mall in Washington, D.C., to honor the 5,000 African Americans who played a significant role during the American Revolution. In 1985, three descendents of American Revolutionary War patriots formed the foundation because they believed the history of black participation in the war was not well known and that African American soldiers' dedication to liberty and freedom was worthy of recognition in the form of a national memorial. The monument will be located between the Washington Monument and the Lincoln memorial. One wall will feature a 90-foot bronze sculpture and the other wall will contain a narrative describing the contributions of the many slaves and freed African Americans who chose to fight against the British for the freedom of the colonies. Congress supported this endeavor and passed a resolution that authorizes the Foundation to build the monument, and the project is scheduled for completion in 2005. For more information visit the Black Revolutionary War Patriots Foundation website at *www.blackpatriots.org*. Teachers may consider asking students to design a just memorial to black soldiers who fought in the American Revolution.

Primary Source Materials for Lesson 2

2.2.1

Resolution passed by the Massachusetts Committee of Safety, May 1775

Resolved, That is the opinion of this Committee, as the contest now between Great Britain and the Colonies respects the liberties and privileges of the latter, which the Colonies are determined to maintain that the admission of any persons, as soldiers, into the army now raising, but only such as are freemen, will be inconsistent with the principles that are to be supported, and reflect dishonor on this Colony, and that no slaves be admitted into this army upon any consideration whatever.

2.2.2

Council of War proposal, October 8, 1775

Whether it will be advisable to enlist any Negroes in the new army? Or whether there be a distinction between such as are slaves and those who are free?

    It was agreed unanimously to reject all slaves; and, by a great majority, to reject Negroes altogether.

2.2.3

Letter from George Washington to Nicholas Cooke, January 2, 1778

Head Quarters, January 2, 1778.

    Sir: Inclosed you will receive a Copy of a Letter from Genl. Varnum to me, upon the means which might be adopted for completing the Rhode Island Troops to their full proportion in the Continental Army. I have nothing to say, in addition to what I wrote the 29th of last Month on this important subject, but to desire that you will give the Officers employed in this business all the assistance in your power. I am, etc.

2.2.4

Response by Massachusetts legislature to a petition for a colored regiment, 1778

STATE OF MASSACHUSETTS BAY:
The Committee of both Houses upon the letter of THOMAS KENCH, with other papers accompanying it, have attended to that service, and report—

That there be one regiment of volunteers raised, as soon as possible, to serve during the war, to consist of the same number of officers and privates as those of a continental regiment;—That one sergeant in each company, and every higher officer in said regiment, shall be white men, and that all the other sergeants, inferior officers and privates shall be negroes, mulattoes, or Indians.

The full text of Document 2.2.4 is available on the CD-ROM.

2.2.5

Letter from Alexander Hamilton to John Jay, President of Congress, March 14, 1779

Dear Sir: Colonel Laurens, who will have the honor of delivering you this letter, is on his way to South Carolina, on a project which I think, in the present situation of affairs there, is a very good one, and deserves every kind of support and encouragement. This is, to raise two, three, or four battalions of negroes, with the assistance of the government of that State, by contributions from the owners, in proportion to the number they possess. If you should think proper to enter upon the subject with him, he will give you a detail of his plan. He wishes to have it recommended by Congress to the State; and, as an inducement, that they would engage to take their battalions into Continental pay.

It appears to me, that an expedient of this kind, in the present state of Southern affairs, is the most rational that can be adopted, and promises very important advantages. Indeed, I hardly see how a sufficient force can be collected in that quarter without it: and the enemy's operations there are growing infinitely serious and formidable.

The full text of Document 2.2.5 is available on the CD-ROM.

2.2.6

Excerpts from letters exchanged between George Washington and Henry Laurens, March 1779

Dear Sir: . . . The policy of our arming Slaves is, in my opinion, a moot point, unless the enemy set the example; for should we begin to form Battalions of them,

I have not the smallest doubt (if the War is to be prosecuted) of their following us in it, and justifying the measure upon our own ground; the upshot then must be, who can arm fastest, and where are our Arms? besides, I am not clear that a discrimination will not render Slavery more irksome to those who remain in it; most of the good and evil things of this life are judged of by comparison; and I fear a comparison in this case will be productive of much discontent in those who are held in servitude; but as this is a subject that has never employed much of my thoughts, these are no more than the first crude Ideas that have struck me upon the occasion.

The full text of Document 2.2.6 is available on the CD-ROM.

2.2.7

Excerpts from a Congressional Committee resolution, March 29, 1779

That the said negroes be formed into separate corps, as battalions, according to the arrangements adopted for the main army, to be commanded by white commissioned and non-commissioned officers . . .

Resolved, That Congress will make provision for paying the proprietors of such negroes as shall be enlisted for the service of the United States during the war, a full compensation for the property, at a rate not exceeding one thousand dollars for each active, able-bodied negro man of standard size, not exceeding thirty-five years of age, who shall be so enlisted and pass muster.

That no pay or bounty be allowed to the said negroes; but that they be clothed and subsisted at the expense of the United States.

That every negro, who shall well and faithfully serve as a soldier to the end of the present war, and shall then return his arms, be emancipated, and receive the sum of fifty dollars . . . .

The full text of Document 2.2.7 is available on the CD-ROM.

2.2.8

Excerpts from an act of the Rhode Island legislature, February 1778

It is Voted and Resolved, That every able-bodied negro, mulatto, or Indian man-slave in this State may enlist into either of the said two battalions, to serve during the continuance of the present war with Great Britain; That every slave so enlisting shall be entitled to and receive all the bounties, wages and encouragements allowed by the Continental Congress to any soldiers enlisting into this service.

It in further Voted and Resolved, That every slave so enlisting shall, upon his passing muster by Col. Christopher Greene, be immediately discharged from the service of his master or mistress, and be absolutely free, as though he had never been incumbered and be incumbered with any kind of servitude or slavery. And in case such slave shall, by sickness or otherwise, be rendered unable to maintain himself, he shall not be chargeable to his master or mistress, but shall be supported at the expense of the State . . . .

The full text of Document 2.2.8 is available on the CD-ROM.

2.2.9

Image of "Hope," the First Rhode Island Continental Regiment flag

"Hope" is the Rhode Island state motto.

Courtesy of Pennsylvania Sons of the Revolution

2.2.10

Excerpt from a speech by Governor Eustis of Massachusetts on the First Rhode Island Regiment, December 12, 1820

In Rhode Island, where their numbers were more considerable, they were formed, under the same considerations, into a regiment commanded by white officers, and it is required in justice to them to add that they discharged their duty with zeal and fidelity. The gallant defense of Red Bank, in which this black regiment bore a part, is among the proofs of their valor. Among the traits that distinguish this regiment was their devotion to their officers; when their brave Colonel Greene was afterwards cut down and mortally wounded, the sabres of the enemy reached his body only through the limbs of his faithful guard of blacks, who hovered over him, and protected him, every one of whom was killed, and whom he was not ashamed to call his children. The services of this description of men in the navy is also well known.

The full text of Document 2.2.10 is available on the CD-ROM.

2.2.11

Excerpts from an address delivered in 1842 before the Congregational and Presbyterian Anti-Slavery Society at Francestown, New Hampshire, by Dr. Harris, a Revolutionary War veteran and member of the First Rhode Island Regiment

When stationed in the State of Rhode Island, the regiment to which I belonged was once ordered to what was called a flanking position,—that is, upon a place which the enemy must pass in order to come round in our rear, to drive us from the fort. This pass was every thing, both to them and to us; of course, it was a post of imminent danger. They attacked us with great fury, but were repulsed. They reinforced, and attacked us again, with more vigor and determination, and again were repulsed. Again they reinforced, and attacked us the third time, with the most desperate courage and resolution, but a third time were repulsed. The contest was fearful. Our position was hotly disputed and as hotly maintained.

The full text of Document 2.2.11 is available on the CD-ROM.

2.2.12

Image of the Marquis de Lafayette at Yorktown, attended by James Armistead Lafayette

During the Revolutionary War, James Armistead volunteered for service with General Lafayette. Pretending he was a runaway, Armistead worked as a spy behind British lines. Later he worked as a servant in Cornwallis's camp and relayed information back to Lafayette. In tribute to General Lafayette, James Armistead adopted the surname Lafayette and used it the rest of his life.

"Lafayette at Yorktown" by Jean-Baptiste le Paon

Courtesy of Lafayette College Art Collection, Easton, PA

2.2.13

Image of James Armistead Lafayette and testimonial by the Marquis de Lafayette

General Lafayette returned to the United States in 1784 and wrote the testimonial about James Armistead's service on behalf of the Patriot cause. This was instrumental in helping the enslaved man gain his freedom from the Virginia General Assembly three years later. In 1824, Richmond artist John Blennerhasset Martin created this broadside, with the likeness of James Armistead Lafayette and the text from General Lafayette.

This is to certify that the bearer by the name of James has done essential services to me while I had the honour to command in this state. His intelligences from the enemy's camp were industriously collected and faithfully delivered. He perfectly acquitted himself with some important commissions I gave him and appears to me entitled to every reward his situation can admit of. Done under my hand, Richmond, November 21st, 1784.

Lafayette

Courtesy of Lafayette College
Special Collections and Archives

2.2.14

Eulogy of James Forten, delivered by Robert Purvis, March 30, 1842

In this cruise, however, they were unfortunate; for, falling in with three of the enemy's vessels,—the *Amphyon, Nymph,* and *Pomona,*—they were forced to strike their colors, and become prisoners of war. It was at this juncture that his mind was harassed with the most painful forebodings, from a knowledge of the fact that rarely, if ever, were prisoners of his complexion exchanged; they were sent to the West Indies, and there doomed to a life of slavery. But his destiny, by a kind Providence, was otherwise. He was placed on board the *Amphyon*, Captain Beasly, who, struck with his open and honest countenance, made him the companion of his son. During one of those dull and monotonous periods which frequently occur on ship-board, young Beasly and Forten were engaged in a game at marbles, when, with signal dexterity and skill, the marbles were upon every trial successively displaced by the unerring hand of Forten. This excited the surprise and admiration of his young companion, who, hastening to his father, called his attention to it. Upon being questioned as to the truth of the matter, and assuring the Captain that nothing was easier for him to accomplish, the marbles were again placed in the ring, and in rapid succession he redeemed his word . . . .

The full text of Document 2.2.14 is available on the CD-ROM.

2.2.15

Excerpt from *The Colored Patriots of the American Revolution: With Sketches of Several Distinguished Colored Persons: To Which Is Added a Brief Survey of the Condition And Prospects of Colored Americans* by William Cooper Nell, 1855

His name is OLIVER CROMWELL, and he says that he was born at the Black Horse, (now Columbus,) in this county, in the family of John Hutchin. He enlisted in company commanded by Capt. Lowery, attached to the Second New Jersey Regiment, under the command of Col. Israel Shreve. He was at the battles of Trenton, Princeton, Brandywine, Monmouth, and Yorktown, at which latter place, he told us, he saw the last man killed. Although his faculties are failing, yet he relates many interesting reminiscences of the Revolution. He was with the army at the retreat of the Delaware, on the memorable crossing of the 25th of December, 1776, and relates the story of the battles on the succeeding days with enthusiasm. He gives the details of the march from Trenton to Princeton, and told us, with much humor, that they "knocked the British about lively" at the latter place. He was also at the battle of Springfield, and says that he saw the house burning in which Mrs. Caldwell was shot, at Connecticut Farms.

The full text of Document 2.2.15 is available on the CD-ROM.

2.2.16

Image of Oliver Cromwell's discharge signed by George Washington

Courtesy of the National Archives

2.2.17

Letters by Charles Sedgewick and Agrippa Hull to Acting Secretary of State Richard Rush, June 12, 1828

Sir, I percieve by an advertisement of yours in [. . .], Register that the pensioners of the U.S. claiming under the Law of 1828 can (if allowed) have their money transmitted to them at the place of their residence. I am reluctant to impose any unnecessary burden upon your department, but am induced by the wish to serve one of the most respectable survivors of the Rev. army, a colored man to avail myself of the privilege there offered to request that his money may be transmitted to him at Stockbridge by mail (an order if convenient on some Bank in Boston or N. York)—I enclose his discharge and take the liberty to request that it may be returned—and also to mention as an interesting fact in regard to this man that I have obtained his permission to send it with great difficulty. He declaims that he had rather forego the pension than lose the discharge.—

Lenox June 12. 1828.
I am Sir, with great respect
Yours [. . .]
Cha. Sedgewick

The full text of Document 2.2.17 is available on the CD-ROM.

2.2.18

Petition on behalf of Salem Poor, December 1775

The subscribers begg leave, to Report to your Honorable House (which wee do in justice to the caracter of so Brave a Man), that, under Our Own observation, Wee declare that a Negro Man, called Salem Poor, of Col. Fryes regiment, Capt. Ames company, in the late Battle of Charlestown, behaved like an Experienced officer, as well as an Excellent Soldier, to set forth Particulars of his conduct would be tedious, Wee Would Only begg leave to say in the Person of this said Negro Centers a brave and gallant soldier. The Reward due to so great and Distinguisht a Caracter, Wee Submit to the Congress.
   Cambridge, Dec. 5, 1775

The full text of Document 2.2.18 is available on the CD-ROM.

2.2.19

Excerpt from "Sketches of Bunker Hill Battle," by Samuel Swett, 1818, from William Cooper Nell's *The Colored Patriots of the American Revolution*, 1855

Swett, in his "Sketches of Bunker Hill Battle," states:—Major Pitcairn caused the first effusion of blood at Lexington. In that battle, his horse was shot under him, while he was separated from his troops. With presence of mind, he feigned himself slain; his pistols were taken from his holsters, and he was left for dead, when he seized the opportunity, and escaped. He appeared at Bunker Hill, and, says the historian, 'Among those who mounted the works was the gallant Major Pitcairn, who exultingly cried out, "*The day is ours*!" when a black soldier named SALEM shot him through, and he fell. His agonized son received him in his arms, and tenderly bore him to the boats.' A contribution was made in the army for the colored soldier, and he was presented to Washington as having performed this feat.

LESSON 2: AFRICAN AMERICANS IN THE AMERICAN REVOLUTION

2.2.20

Image of Peter Salem at Bunker Hill, from William Cooper Nell's *The Colored Patriots of the American Revolution*, 1855

Boston-born William Cooper Nell (1816–74) was in the forefront of desegregation efforts in the city's schools, performance halls, and on the railroads. In 1851, he became the first published black historian, when he wrote Services of Colored Americans in the Wars of 1776 and 1812. *Four years later, he followed with* The Colored Patriots of the American Revolution. *Nell is also distinguished as the first African American to hold a federal civilian post. From 1861 until his death he worked as a U.S. postal clerk.*

2.2.21

Drawing by Henry Pelham of Crispus Attucks in the Boston Massacre, 1770

This drawing of the so-called Boston Massacre was created by Henry Pelham and published nearly two weeks after Paul Revere's image. Pelham was the stepbrother of John Singleton Copley.

Courtesy of Corbis Images

LESSON 2: AFRICAN AMERICANS IN THE AMERICAN REVOLUTION

2.2.22

Engraving by Paul Revere of Boston Massacre, 1770

Paul Revere (1735–1818), silversmith and patriot, is best known for his ride from Boston to Lexington on the night of April 18, 1775, to warn colonists that British troops were coming. Just as Henry Wadsworth Longfellow got details of Revere's ride wrong (he never made it to Concord), so too did Revere miss details in his engraving of the "massacre."

Courtesy of the Library of Congress

LESSON 3

The Black Loyalists—Emigrants to a New Life

During the American Revolution, enslaved African Americans found a variety of ways to gain their freedom. One important route was through service to the British. The British did not intend to abolish the institution of slavery in their colonies, but they knew that offering slaves freedom in exchange for labor would give them an important advantage and deprive the Continentals (as the rebellious Americans were then known) of a key resource. They understood that the Continental war effort was financed by plantation owners, such as Jefferson and Washington, whose wealth was built in large measure on the labor of slaves. The first British offer of freedom was made to slaves in Virginia.

John Earl of Dunmore, governor of the Virginia colony, fled the capital, Williamsburg, which was in the hands of Patriots (as they called themselves), to the safety of a British ship in the harbor of Norfolk. Needing additional soldiers and seeking to undermine the Patriot economy, Dunmore made a dramatic proclamation in November 1775: he promised freedom to any enslaved persons who would desert their masters and serve the Loyalist cause. As the news traveled throughout Virginia and beyond, some black mothers named their newborns "Dunmore." Dunmore's strategy did not stem from any moral or religious objections to slavery; as governor, he had withheld his signature from a bill outlawing the slave trade. His motives, however, did not matter to African Americans who chose this route to freedom. More than three thousand black people eventually joined the British, despite their concern about possible reprisals against the family members they left behind.

Dunmore created a short-lived battalion of men called the Ethiopian Regiment, whose uniforms were emblazoned with the words Liberty to Slaves. Other black military units established during the course of the war included the Black Pioneers and Guides, the Jersey and Mosquito Shore Volunteers, the King's American Dragoons, the Jamaica Rangers, and the Black Brigade, a guerilla-style force. Thousands of other men, women, and children cooked, sewed, built buildings, dug trenches, and carried water for British troops.

Some Loyalist slaveholders fled to England and abandoned their plantation households, leaving slaves to fend for themselves. In other cases, advancing or retreating British armies came upon black people who joined their ranks and remained under their protection. In 1779, British General Sir Henry Clinton issued the Philipsburg Proclamation, expanding Dunmore's Proclamation to include any slaves who could escape to British lines, whether or not they were ready to serve the British army, anywhere in the colonies.

According to the 1783 Treaty of Paris, which ended the war, African Americans who could prove that they had been behind British lines for at least a year before the treaty were issued a Certificate of Freedom. American negotiators, worried that so much of their "property" had been "confiscated," demanded that the British government guarantee financial compensation to all Americans whose slaves had joined the British. This issue remained unresolved until 1826, when the British Treasury settled war claims by paying one million pounds for 3,601 people.

Many African Americans who sought freedom behind British lines eventually found refuge in New York City, along with 40,000 other Loyalists who were seeking safety. Sir Guy Carleton was in charge of the British withdrawal of troops and civilians from New York to various locations in the British Empire, including Canada, the West Indies, and England. He withstood strong pressure from General Washington and others to return former slaves who had escaped from American owners. The British government stood by its commitments.

Before refugees were transported from New York, both black and white evacuees were carefully registered. A detailed log, called the "Book of Negroes," identified where people originally came from and who had owned them. This log records a number of intact families, with mother, father, and children—relationships that are often not apparent in other documents of enslaved people in British North America.

Many of the Loyalists of African descent were evacuated to Nova Scotia in 1783, with high hopes for the future and promises of land grants and provisions to get started. One of the first towns settled by black Loyalists was named Birchtown, after the general who had signed their Certificates of Freedom. But the harsh climate, limited resources, and racist attitudes they encountered made Nova Scotia a difficult place for black people. Some white Loyalists actually brought enslaved workers with them; chattel slavery was legal in the British colonies until 1834. Free blacks in Nova Scotia—like those in many of the states—were discriminated against and treated as cheap labor.

Most African Americans who settled in Nova Scotia were from the southern states. Their skills in cultivating tobacco, cotton, and rice were of little use in this bleak, northern land. Black Loyalists faced greater difficulties than white people, who had simply to adapt to the environment. African Americans were the last to receive land and provisions; when supplies were short, they received nothing. Most relied on what they could obtain from the forest. Although thousands of feet of cut lumber were exported from Nova Scotia, black Loyalists in Birchtown lived in simple huts with wicker walls and roofs tied together in a cone and covered in birch bark—reminiscent of African and Native American dwellings. Oral histories also mention dugouts with roofs of cloth and tree boughs. This type of hut was commonly used as temporary housing by the military because it was quickly and easily built. But such dwellings were ill-suited for permanent, year-round residences in a cold climate.

In 1792, after almost a decade of trying to build farms on poor land and enduring starvation conditions, black Loyalists were offered another chance to build a new home, this time in the British colony of Sierra Leone, West Africa. More than 1,200 members of the community responded to the opportunity; these families became the founders of Freetown in 1793. Prominent among the emigrants were religious leaders, such as John Marrant, David George, and Boston King. Others, such as Thomas Peters, were former military men. In Africa, as in Canada, refugees encountered broken promises, racist attitudes, and government structures that did nor allow them full participation in economic and political decision making. Nonetheless, some families in Freetown, as in Nova Scotia, proudly trace their ancestors back to enslaved people who left plantations in Virginia and the Carolinas to seek freedom.

Organizing Idea

The American War of Independence continued the African diaspora, leading black people to many parts of the British Empire and resulting in the founding of Freetown, Sierra Leone. The British offered African Americans freedom in exchange for labor and resettled them after their defeat. Black people seeking freedom took risks and endured difficult conditions in their quest for better lives.

Student Objectives

Students will:

- ❖ map the route traveled by some enslaved people from Virginia, the Carolinas, and other colonies to ports in Nova Scotia and then across the Atlantic to Freetown, Sierra Leone, in West Africa
- ❖ recognize the military and economic interests that led the British to offer freedom to black Loyalists during the Revolutionary War and yet continue slavery in their colonies
- ❖ use primary sources to learn stories of individual black people who sought freedom from slavery

Key Questions

- ❖ How did people of African descent enslaved in the English colonies use the disruptions and opportunities presented by the Revolutionary War to escape from slavery?
- ❖ What can primary sources teach us about the choices African Americans faced and the paths they traveled in search of freedom and a decent home during and after the War for Independence?
- ❖ To what degree and in what ways did African Americans attain their goals by moving to Nova Scotia and Sierra Leone?

Lesson 3: The Black Loyalists—Emigrants to a New Life

Primary Source Materials

DOCUMENT 2.3.1: The Earl of Dunmore's Proclamation, 1775

DOCUMENT 2.3.2: Image of the runaway advertisement for Titus, November 8, 1775

DOCUMENT 2.3.3: Image of the extract of a letter from Monmouth County, New Jersey, June 12, 1780, regarding Colonel Ty

DOCUMENT 2.3.4: Virginia Declaration, December 1775

DOCUMENT 2.3.5: Excerpt from "An Account of [the] life of Mr. David George given by himself. In a conversation with Brother Rippon of London and Brother Pearce in Birmingham," 1790s

DOCUMENT 2.3.6: Excerpt from "King's Memoir," by Boston King, June 1796

DOCUMENT 2.3.7: Image of Cato Hamanday's Certificate of Freedom signed by British General Birch, 1783

DOCUMENT 2.3.8: Two-page transcription from the "Book of Negroes," 1783

DOCUMENT 2.3.9: Excerpt from the diary of British officer William Dyott, 1788

DOCUMENT 2.3.10: "Free Settlement on the Coast of Africa," handbill, 1791

Supplementary Materials

ITEM 2.3.A: Additional vocabulary lists for primary sources

ITEM 2.3.B: Map of Atlantic World

Vocabulary

abettors	forfeiture	"His Majesty's tenders"	martial law
able-bodied	guineas (British colonial money)	"hue and cry"	proclamation
accommodation		insurrection	treason
confiscation			

Student Activities

Reading and Analysis of Documents Relating to Conditions in 1775

Activity 1

In small groups, read Lord Dunmore's 1775 Proclamation (2.3.1), the Virginia Assembly's 1775 response (2.3.4), and the excerpt from David George's memoir of his early days in Virginia (2.3.5) Answer the guiding questions for each and then discuss with your group what you consider to be the most significant points regarding the document as whole.

Document 2.3.1: Dunmore's Proclamation

❖ Where is Lord Dunmore when he makes this Proclamation?

❖ How does Lord Dunmore describe the people of the Virginia Colony?

- How does Lord Dunmore describe the situation in the colony?
- By what "authority" does Lord Dunmore have the ability to offer freedom to indentured servants and Negroes?

Document 2.3.4: The Virginia Declaration

- Where are the representatives of the people of the Virginia Colony when they make this Declaration?
- How do they describe the people of the Virginia Colony, both free and enslaved?
- How do they describe the effects of Lord Dunmore's Proclamation?
- What are the two choices that the General Convention offers to those who have escaped to fight with Lord Dunmore?

Document 2.3.5: Memoir of David George

- Did David George know his family?
- What kind of work did David George do as a young person?
- What kind of man was Mr. Chapel?

Activity 2   Examining Images—One Black Man's Story

Have students examine the images of the runaway slave advertisement (2.3.2) and the excerpt from the letter (2.3.3). Alert students to the old use of the letter "f" as an "s" so they can understand the words. Then discuss:

- How do these two primary source documents fit with Lord Dunmore's Proclamation (2.3.1)?
- Is there anything surprising in either document?
- How do primary sources, such as these, help us understand the diverse roles of African Americans in the American Revolution?
- Why might Titus and many other enslaved blacks have joined the British in 1775 and not the Patriot side?

Activity 3   Examining Documents—Exodus from New York

Organize the class into three groups. Study the excerpt from Boston King's memoir (2.3.6) General Birch's Certificate of Freedom for Cato Hamanday (2.3.7), and the two pages from the sixty-page British document, "The Book of Negroes" (2.3.8). Answer the guiding questions for each document, and then discuss with your group what you consider to be the most significant points. Ask the group to agree on the two most important points to present to the rest of the class, and explain your reasons why.

LESSON 3: THE BLACK LOYALISTS—EMIGRANTS TO A NEW LIFE

Document 2.3.6: The Memoir of Boston King

- What frightening rumor did black people hear in New York City in 1783?
- What horrors did people witness and what impact did that have on them?
- How did the British government make good on its promise to the escaped people?

Document 2.3.7: Cato Hamanday's Certificate of Freedom signed by British General Birch

- What did a person have to do to receive a certificate of freedom?
- This certificate made those who held it legally free from bondage. In what words does the certificate state that?

Document 2.3.8: "Book of Negroes"

- How many ships are listed on these pages and where are they headed?
- Which colonies do most of the people listed come from? List the colonies.
- What is the average age of the people listed here? Are there any children? If there are, are they alone or with their parents?
- What does the phrase "formerly the property of" mean?

Reading—Life in Nova Scotia and Beyond

Activity 4

Discuss the natural environment (bad farmland, extremely cold winters, rocky, swampy) and economic situations (last to receive provisions, good land given to others, last hired–first fired) that greeted the Black Loyalists in Nova Scotia. Give each student a copy of the excerpt from British officer William Dyott's brief description of Birchtown (2.3.9) and the handbill, "Free Settlement on the Coast of Africa," inviting Black Loyalists to settle in Sierra Leone (2.3.10). Ask the class to read the guiding questions and to answer them as a group. Discuss the significance of each as a whole class.

Document 2.3.9: William Dyott's Diary

- Why do you think the Black Loyalists named this community "Birch Town"?
- How many years after the departure from New York did Dyott visit Birch Town?
- Does Birch Town seem like a good place to live? How would you describe it?

Document 2.3.10: Handbill

- What does the Sierra Leone Company offer to free blacks?
- For what does the Company ask in exchange for what they are offering?
- What is most significant about the proposed way that black and white people will be treated?

- ❖ The brochure talks about an Act of Parliament and the Company's ability to "deal or traffic in the buying or selling of Slaves . . ." Why do you think they included that paragraph?

Activity 5

Mapping—Black Loyalists' Journeys

Choose one of the families listed in the "Book of Negroes" excerpt (2.3.8) and use your map (Item 2.3.B) to trace the journey from the colonial English plantation from which they came to New York City and then to the port in Nova Scotia, where their ship was sent. Be sure to include the name of the ship and the date of departure. From our documents, we don't know exactly which families chose to leave for Sierra Leone, but we know that many did. On your map, trace the journey to Freetown, Sierra Leone.

Activity 6

Essay Writing—Hopes of Enslaved People

Write a brief essay: People of African descent who left their plantations in the southern colonies to go behind British lines were hoping to achieve something. Based on the documents, what do you think that was, and do you feel they succeeded?

Activity 7

Research extension—Story of a Black Loyalist

Research Black Loyalist websites (listed in Further Resources) to identify a person or family that interests you. Make a presentation with words and images that tells their story. The history of the early settlers to Freetown, Sierra Leone, provides another great story of perseverance in the face of extreme obstacles. Research it. You can use the materials compiled by Mary Louise Clifford as a starting point.

Further Student and Teacher Resources

Clifford, Mary Louise. *From Slavery to Freetown: Black Loyalists After the American Revolution.* Jefferson, NC and London: McFarland & Co., Inc., 1999.

Mckerrow, P. E. Edited by Frank Stanley Boyd. *A Brief History of the Coloured Baptists of Nova Scotia 1783–1895.* Halifax, NS: Afro-Nova Scotian Enterprises, 1975.

Pulis, John W. *Moving On: Black Loyalists in the Afro-Atlantic World.* Garland Publishing, 1999.

Robertson, Marion. *King's Bounty: A History of Early Shelburne Nova Scotia.* Halifax, NS: Museum Press, 1983.

Smith, T. Watson. *"The Slave in Canada," Collections of the Nova Scotia Historical Society for the Years 1896–98 Volume X.* Halifax, NS: Nova Scotia Printing Company, 1899.

Walker, James W. St. G. *The Black Loyalists: The Search for a Promised Land in Nova Scotia and Sierra Leone.* Toronto, ON: University of Toronto Press, 1976.

Winks, Robin W. *The Blacks in Canada: A History,* 2d ed. Montreal and Kingston: McGill-Queens University Press, 1997.

Websites

http://collections.ic.gc.ca/blackloyalists/ *Part of Canada's "digital collections" websites. This site can easily provide the material for many other lessons. Full of extensively researched and illustrated information, the site explores the story of Canada's first settlements of free blacks outside Africa and includes many primary source documents.*

http://museum.gov.ns.ca/blackloyalists/index.htm *Among many excellent primary source images that span the years 1750–2000, this site also contains a 45-min. web-based student detective archaeological activity: "Was this the house of Colonel Stephen Blucke?" Blucke was a leader of the Birchtown Black Loyalist community in Nova Scotia. A seventeen-page resource packet includes complete student handouts for groups of four with many eighteenth-century primary sources (printable .pdf file). For those interested in genealogical research, there is also an indexed list of Black Loyalist surnames recovered during a 1998–1999 research project.*

Contemporary Connection
※

Loyalist Descendants

The Black Cultural Society of Nova Scotia (*www.bccns.com*) keeps African Canadian heritage alive in the Maritimes. Its website provides historical information covering several waves of Canadian immigration of peoples of African descent, including the 1796 arrival of 550 Jamaican exiles and the British refugees from the War of 1812. Later arrivals flocked to Cape Breton from the Caribbean during the 1920s to work in coal mines and the steel factory. The website features links to history, music, heroes, stories, and upcoming events. There are also links to other related sites, such as the Black Loyalist Society.

Ask students to discover when African Americans settled in their town or city. Did they arrive as early as the 1600s, or as black pioneers in the late 1700s, or with other migrations in the nineteenth or twentieth century? Gathering stories from local residents enriches and deepens the history of local communities.

Primary Source Materials for Lesson 3

2.3.1

The Earl of Dunmore's Proclamation, 1775

I do require every Person capable of bearing Arms, to resort to His MAJESTY'S STANDARD, or be looked upon as Traitors to His MAJESTY'S Crown and Government, and thereby become liable to the Penalty the Law inflicts upon such Offenses; such as forfeiture of Life, confiscation of Lands, &. &. And I do hereby further declare all indented Servants, Negroes, or others, (appertaining to Rebels,) free that are able and willing to bear Arms, they joining His MAJESTY'S Troops as soon as may be . . .

The full text of Document 2.3.1 is available on the CD-ROM.

LESSON 3: THE BLACK LOYALISTS—EMIGRANTS TO A NEW LIFE 57

2.3.2

Image of the runaway advertisement for Titus, November 8, 1775

Titus was one of four African Americans owned by Quaker John Corlies of Shrewsbury, New Jersey. Titus fled from his master the day after Dunmore's Proclamation and joined British forces. As his former owner surmised, Titus did change his name. Although never formally commissioned by the British army, he was widely known as Colonel Tye.

> **THREE POUNDS Reward.**
> RUN away from the subscriber, living in Shrewsbury, in the county of Monmouth, New-Jersey, a NEGROE man, named TITUS, but may probably change his name; he is about 21 years of age, not very black, near 6 feet high; had on a grey homespun coat, brown breeches, blue and white stockings, and took with him a wallet, drawn up at one end with a string, in which was a quantity of clothes. Whoever takes up said Negroe, and secures him in any goal, or brings him to me, shall be entitled to the above reward of *Three Pounds* proc. and all reasonable charges, paid by
> Nov. 8, 1775. § JOHN CORLIS.

2.3.3

Image of the extract of a letter from Monmouth County, New Jersey, June 12, 1780, regarding Colonel Ty

Within a week of Dunmore's proclamation, more than three hundred slaves fled to the British army in Norfolk, Virginia. In subsequent weeks, blacks seeking freedom came by the hundreds. Dunmore formed the Royal Ethiopian Regiment. Titus, who became known as "Colonel Tye" (or Ty), was one of its most respected fighters, famous for his guerrilla-style attacks on Patriot supplies and forces. He died in action in 1780.

> *Extract of a letter from Monmouth county, June 12.*
> "Ty, with his party of about 20 blacks and whites, last Friday afternoon took and carried off prisoners, Capt. Barns Smock and Gilbert Vanmater; at the same time spiked up the iron four pounder at Capt. Smock's house, but took no ammunition: Two of the artillery horses, and two of Capt. Smock's horses, were likewise taken off."
> The above-mentioned Ty is a Negroe, who bears the title of Colonel, and commands a motly crew at Sandy-Hook.

2.3.4

Virginia Declaration, December 1775

A DECLARATION

WHEREAS lord Dunmore, by his proclamation, dated on board the ship *William*, off Norfolk, the 7th day of November 1775, hath offered freedom to such able-bodied slaves as are willing to join him, and take up arms, against the good people of this colony, giving thereby encouragement to a general insurrection, which may induce a necessity of inflicting the severest punishments upon those unhappy people, already deluded by his base and insidious arts; and whereas, by an act of the General Assembly now in force in this colony, it is enacted, that all negro or other slaves, conspiring to rebel or make insurrection, shall suffer death, and be excluded all benefit of clergy: We think it proper to declare, that all slaves who have been, or shall be seduced, by his lordship's proclamation, or other arts, to desert their masters' service, and take up arms against the inhabitants of this colony, shall be liable to such punishment as shall hereafter be directed by the General Convention. And to that end all such, who have taken this unlawful and wicked step, may return in safety to their duty, and escape the punishment due to their crimes, we hereby promise pardon to them, they surrendering themselves to Col. William Woodford, or any other commander of our troops, and not appearing in arms after the publication hereof. And we do farther earnestly recommend it to all humane and benevolent persons in this colony to explain and make known this our offer of mercy to those unfortunate people.

2.3.5

Excerpt from "An Account of [the] life of Mr. David George given by himself. In a conversation with Brother Rippon of London and Brother Pearce in Birmingham," 1790s

I also have been whipped many a time on my naked skin, and sometimes till the blood has run down over my waistband, but the greatest grief I then had was to see them whip my mother, and to hear her on her knees, begging for mercy. She was master's cook, and if they only thought she might do anything better than she did, instead of speaking to her as to a servant, they would strip her directly and cut away. I believe she was on her deathbed when I got off, but I have never heard since. Master's rough and cruel usage was the reason for my running away . . . I left the plantation about midnight, walked all night, got into Brunswick County, then over Roanoke River, and soon met with some white traveling people, who helped me on to Pedee River. When I had been at work there two or three weeks, A hue and cry found me out, and the master said to me, there are thirty (30) guineas offered for you, but I will have no hand in it. I would advise you to make your way toward Savannah River. I hearkened to him, but was several weeks going.

The full text of Document 2.3.5 is available on the CD-ROM.

2.3.6

Excerpt from "King's Memoir," by Boston King, June 1796

About which time, (in 1783) the horrors and devastation of war happily terminated and peace was restored between America and Great Britain, which diffused universal joy among all parties; except us, who had escaped from slavery and taken refuge in the English army; for a report prevailed at New-York, that all the slaves, in number 2000, were to be delivered up to their masters altho' some of them had been three or four years among the English. This dreadful rumour filled us all with inexpressible anguish and terror, especially when we saw our old masters coming from Virginia, North Carolina, and other parts, and seizing upon their slaves in the streets of New York, or even dragging them out of their beds. Many of the slaves had very cruel masters, so that the thoughts of returning home with them embittered life to us. For some days we lost our appetite for food, and sleep departed from our eyes. The English had compassion upon us in the day of distress, and issued out a Proclamation, importing, That all slaves should be free, who had taken refuge in the British lines, and claimed the sanction and privileges of the Proclamations respecting the security and protection of Negroes.

The full text of Document 2.3.6 is available on the CD-ROM.

2.3.7

Image of Cato Hamanday's Certificate of Freedom signed by British General Birch, 1783

British authorities issued certificates of freedom, proof that former slaves had joined them before the provisional treaty was signed in 1782. These certificates prevented former masters from reclaiming their "property" and allowed blacks passage out of the United States.

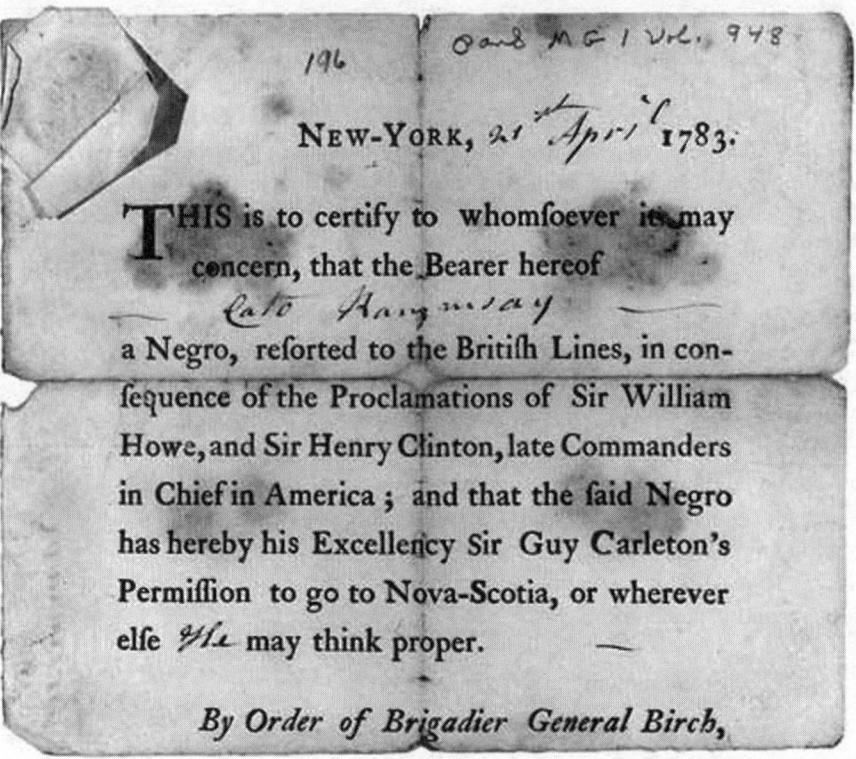

Courtesy of Nova Scotia Archives and Records Management

2.3.8

Two-page transcription from the "Book of Negroes," 1783

29 July 1783
Stafford bound for Port Roseway—Robert Watson

Name	Age	Description	Formerly the Property of	Escape	GBC (yes/no)	Further Info.
Bill Williams	19	stout lad	John Frazer of White Bluff, GA	4 years ago	yes	
Peter Johnson	18	stout lad	William Johnson of Wilmington, NC	2 years ago	yes	
John Ranger	24	stout fellow	James Wright by certificate from David Matthews, Mayor of NY		no	
William Williams	23	stout fellow	Col Warrington of NC	3 years ago	yes	

The full text of Document 2.3.8 is available on the CD-ROM.

2.3.9

Excerpt from the diary of British officer William Dyott, 1788

Dyott and fellow officers . . . —walked through the woods about two miles from the barracks to a negro town called Birch Town. At the evacuation of New York there were a great number of these poor devils given lands and settled here—The place is beyond description wretched, situated on the coast in the middle of barren rocks, and partly surrounded by a thick impenetrable wood—Their huts miserable to guard against the inclemency of a Nova Scotia winter, and their existence almost depending on what they could lay up in summer. I think I never saw wretchedness and poverty so strongly perceptible in the garb and the countenance of the human species as in these miserable outcasts. I cannot say I was sorry to quit so melancholy a dwelling.

2.3.10

"Free Settlement on the Coast of Africa," handbill, 1791.

That every Free Black (upon producing such a Certificate) shall have a Grant of not less than Twenty Acres of Land for himself, Ten for his wife, and five for every child, upon such terms and subject to such changes and obligations, (with a view to the general prosperity of the Company) as shall hereafter be settled by the Company, in respect to the Grants of Lands to be made by them to all Settlers, whether black or white.

That for all stores, provisions, or, supplied from the Company's Warehouse, the company shall receive an equitable compensation, according to fixed rules, extending to blacks and whites indeterminately.

That the civil, military, personal, and commercial rights and duties of Blacks and Whites, shall be the same, and secured in the same manner.

The full text of Document 2.3.10 is available on the CD-ROM.

LESSON 4

Massachusetts Abolishes Slavery, 1783

From the British colonial era to the Civil War, two communities of African Americans grew up in this country. One was enslaved, the other free. In all the British colonies, African Americans had to confront the reality of communal fragmentation as well as that of racial differentiation. Because there was no crowd in which to mask their racial features, they were set apart by the dominant white American society and marked for unequal treatment.

Prior to the Declaration of Independence and the ratification of the Constitution, some slaves successfully sued in the courts to win their emancipation. To secure their freedom, colonial slaves appealed to the legal protections established in British common law, the colonial charters, and, later, in the Massachusetts Bill of Rights. By so doing, these African American forefathers created an enduring tradition for black Americans to pursue and gain their civil rights through judicial recourse.

In 1781, Quok Walker (also referred to as Quock, Quacks, Quack, Quork, and Quork Walker) ran away from Nathaniel Jennison's farm in Massachusetts and took refuge on a farm belonging to Seth and John Caldwell. The men were not strangers; their older brother had originally purchased Walker and his parents in 1754. After the elder Caldwell's death, Quok became the property of his widow, who some time later married Nathaniel Jennison.

Jennison claimed Quok Walker was his property. He and his friends captured Walker, beat him, and forced him to return to the Jennison farm. Within days, Walker filed suit against Jennison for assault and battery. Jennison countersued, claiming that the Caldwell brothers had interfered with his property and that they enticed Walker away for their own benefit. Thus began a series of cases that ultimately challenged the legality of chattel slavery in Massachusetts, using the just-ratified state constitution to support the argument.

For more than two decades preceding the Walker case, Massachusetts juries had frequently found in favor of slaves when they sued for their freedom on the basis of contracts with their owners. In *Quok Walker v. Nathaniel Jennison,* the jury found for the African American, stating that "a Freeman was not the proper Negro slave" of Jennison because Walker's former master had promised his freedom once he reached twenty-five, a promise renewed by Caldwell's widow. They declined to award him the £300 in damages he sought; he got £50.

Nathaniel Jennison appealed the jury decision but lost when he failed to appear in court. However, in the second case, Jennison won. The jury contradicted the first one and awarded Jennison £25. Walker's lawyer appealed the case to the Massachusetts Supreme Judicial Court. He did not refer to the state constitution but claimed that slavery was a violation of the laws of nature and God. The court agreed and overturned the jury's finding.

The final case was a criminal one rather than civil. The Commonwealth of Massachusetts indicted Jennison for assault and battery against Quok Walker. Witnesses again testified that Walker's former master (Caldwell) had promised him freedom. In 1783, the attorney general, trying the case for the state, explained to the jury that this meant that Jennison had attacked a free man. Jennison's lawyer insisted that the Massachusetts constitution of 1789 did not expressly prohibit slavery.

In his instructions to the jury, Chief Justice William Cushing claimed otherwise. He stated that "slavery is in my judgement as effectively abolished as it can be by the granting of rights and privileges wholly incompatible and repugnant to its existence." The jury found Jennison guilty of assault and battery.

Though not set down in law reports, the judge's words and jury's verdict were widely discussed. On the surface, the case was a simple one of assault and battery; however, its legacy is in ending the institution of slavery in the Commonwealth of Massachusetts.

Organizing Idea

African Americans used the colonial courts to achieve emancipation from slavery, appealing first to their "rights as Englishmen" and later to the expectations raised by the Declaration of Independence and the Massachusetts Bill of Rights.

Student Objectives

Students will:

- prepare for and conduct a mock trial
- understand how some slaves used their status as British "subjects," before the American Revolution, to win their freedom by suing their masters and thus asserting their rights under the terms of the royal charters and the English common law
- understand the myriad ways in which enslaved individuals used the judicial system to gain freedom in the early years of the republic
- assess the impact African Americans asserting their rights had on community-building and nation-building and appreciate the influence these actions had, and continue to have, on local, state, and national leaders.

Lesson 4: Massachusetts Abolishes Slavery, 1783

Key Questions

- On what grounds did an enslaved individual sue and win freedom in Massachusetts in 1781?
- What was the impact of the Quok Walker cases on the civil rights of African Americans?
- On what grounds did enslaved individuals in Pennsylvania, Virginia, and North Carolina win their freedom?
- How did various states address the discrepancy between individual rights guaranteed in state and federal constitutions and the institution of slavery?

Primary Source Materials

DOCUMENT 2.4.1: Extract from Chief Justice Cushing's decision in *Quok Walker v. Nathaniel Jennison*, 1783, found in his notebook

DOCUMENT 2.4.2: Chief Justice Cushing's charge to the jury in *Commonwealth [of Massachusetts] v. Jennison*, 1783

DOCUMENT 2.4.3: Excerpts from Justice William Atlee's decision in *Res publica v. Negro Betsey et al.*, Pennsylvania Supreme Court, 1789

DOCUMENT 2.4.4: Excerpts from judge's opinion in *Gobu v. Gobu*, Supreme Court of North Carolina, Hillsborough District, 1802

DOCUMENT 2.4.5: Excerpts from the decision of Supreme Court of Appeals of Virginia in *Hudgins v. Wrights*, 1806

DOCUMENT 2.4.6: Excerpt from Chief Justic Parsons' decision in *Winchendon v. Hatfield*, 1808

Supplementary Materials

ITEM 2.4.A: Additional vocabulary lists for primary sources

Vocabulary

appeal	deposition	marginalized	plethora
attorney	emancipation	nation-	ratify
chattel	*habeas corpus*	building	witness
civil suit	indictment	objectified	
crescendo of	legal challenge	petition	
expectations	manumission	plaintiff	

Student Activities

Activity 1 — **Preparing for the Quok Walker Case**

Students will research and discuss the Quok Walker case. They can begin by reading Judge Cushing's opinion in *Quok Walker v. Nathaniel Jennison* (2.4.1) and Chief Justice Cushing's charge to the jury in *Commonwealth v. Jennison* (2.4.2). They may wish to check online sources and books listed in the resource section.

Students will be assigned roles in the case as follows:

- Chief Justice, the Supreme Judicial Court of Massachusetts
- bailiff
- attorney for Quok Walker
- Mrs. Walker
- attorney for Jennison
- Nathaniel Jennison
- Mrs. Jennison
- eight students as associate justices of the Massachusetts Supreme Judicial Court

Two newspapers will publish each day of the trial (two days). Students may name and format their paper. The staff includes the following:

a. publisher-editor (will editorialize—give opinions—regarding the case)

b. reporter (may state only what happens in court from day to day)

c. political cartoonists (two)

Press conferences are held daily in the minutes preparatory to trial so witnesses and attorneys may be interviewed, photographed, and filmed by the press pool.

Activity 2 — **Writing Assignments Pertaining to Walker's Trial**

All students have writing assignments as follows:

- the judge's opinion
- the attorneys' briefs
- the witnesses' depositions, saying what they know, saw, and heard
- each associate justice's opinion, carefully based on the Massachusetts Bay Charter and/or the Massachusetts Bill of Rights
- the newspaper publishers' daily editorials
- the newspaper reporters' daily articles
- political cartoonists' daily contributions

Multimedia Learning—Images of the Trial

Activity 3

Cameras are permitted in the courtroom and operators are permitted to move around the room during the trial. Images are shared with the press pool for selection in their daily publications.

The Trial

Activity 4

Teachers are the best judges regarding how formal a trial students can conduct. Students come to this activity with a range of experiences regarding court procedure. Television and movies have familiarized many. At *http://projects.edtech.sandi.net/hoover/amistad/#trialprep*, there are general guidelines for a mock trial, although the guide is specifically related to the Amistad case. The central objective is for students to gain an understanding of the issues and arguments involved in Quok Walker's trials.

Reading and Exploring Other Court Cases Challenging Slavery

Activity 5

Working in small groups, with each group assigned a document (2.4.3–2.4.6) related to legal challenges to slavery, students should familiarize themselves with that document. Each team should then prepare a presentation to the entire class explaining the case, clarifying the legal issue involved, and analyzing the impact of that case on the civil rights of African Americans. With the court cases in Virginia and North Carolina in mind, students should discuss, as a class, the issue of race and slavery in the early republic.

The cases are as follows:

- A case from Pennsylvania: *Res publica v. Negro Betsey et al.* (1789). Is a slave child free, if the child was born before the gradual emancipation statutes were enacted in Pennsylvania and, subsequently, was registered improperly (2.4.3)?
- A case from North Carolina, a slave state following the ratification of the Constitution: *Gobu v. Gobu* (1802). Are all blacks presumed to be slaves (2.4.4)?
- A case from Virginia, a slave state following the ratification of the Constitution: *Hudgins v. Wrights* (1806). Are they also slaves who are Africans of mixed Indian blood (2.4.5)?
- Another case from Massachusetts: *Winchendon v. Hatfield* (1808). May a group of slaves sue and win their freedom (2.4.6)?

Further Student and Teacher Resources

Bradley, Patricia. *Slavery, Propaganda and the American Revolution.* Jackson, MS: University Press of Mississippi, 1998.

Kaplan, Sidney, and Emma Nogrady Kaplan. *The Black Presence in the Era of the American Revolution.* Amherst: University of Massachusetts, 1989.

Meltzer, Milton, ed. *The American Revolutionaries: A History in Their Own Words.* New York: HarperCollins, 1993. (middle school)

Quarles, Benjamin. *The Negro in the American Revolution.* Chapel Hill, NC: University of North Carolina Press, 1961.

Contemporary Connection

Using Legal Means in the Twenty-First Century

More than two centuries after the Quok Walker cases were heard in Massachusetts, another precedent-setting series of cases are winding their way through the courts. A team of lawyers, including Charles Ogletree Jr. of Harvard, is taking the government of the United States to court, on behalf of African Americans, for reparations for "slavery and its effects." A secondary goal is to use the legal cases to "stimulate a national debate on the issue," one that Congress has been reluctant to address.

These reparations cases name the federal government or federal agencies as "active participants in causing the harms done by slavery." Arguments center on the government's culpability in taking property and breaking promises. After the Civil War, African Americans believed they had been promised and had earned (through their unpaid labor), 40 acres and a mule, the minimum of property that a Southern farm family would need in order to support themselves. They were bitterly disappointed when the whole plan was officially denied. In Florida and South Carolina, the cases will argue that 40,000 blacks not only did not receive land, but actually lost land previously given to them.

Other cases are also in the works. For example, a case is filed against Tulsa, Oklahoma, for the riot against black people in 1921, and numerous suits have been filed against banks and insurance companies that allegedly profited from the slave trade. Students can use the Internet to discover the latest information about the progress of these various suits. Ask Google for "Reparations Lawsuits."

Primary Source Materials for Lesson 4

2.4.1

Extract from Chief Justice Cushing's decision in *Quok Walker v. Nathaniel Jennison*, 1783, found in his notebook

But whatever sentiments have formerly prevailed in this particular or slid upon us by the example of others, a different idea has taken place with the people of America, more favorable to the natural rights of mankind, and to that natural, innate desire of Liberty, with which Heaven (without regard to color, complexion, or shape of noses-features) has inspired all the human race. And upon this ground our Constitution of Government, by which the people of this Commonwealth have solemnly bound themselves, sets out with declaring that all men are born free and equal—and that every subject is entitled to liberty, and to have it guarded by the laws, as well as life and property—and in short is totally repugnant to the idea of being born slaves. This being the case, I think the idea of slavery is inconsistent with our own conduct and Constitution; and there can be no such thing as perpetual servitude of a rational creature, unless his liberty is forfeited by some criminal conduct or given up by personal consent or contract . . . . *Verdict Guilty*

The full text of Document 2.4.1 is available on the CD-ROM.

2.4.2

Chief Justice Cushing's charge to the jury in *Commonwealth* [of Massachusetts] *v. Jennison*, 1783

In 1781 Nathaniel Jennison was indicted "for an assault on Quack Walker, and beat with a stick 1st May, 1781, and imprisoned two hours." At the end of the trial Chief Justice William Cushing delivered the following charge to the jury.

The defense set up in this case afforded much scope for discussion and has been fully considered. It is founded on the assumed proposition that slavery had been by law established in this province: that rights to slaves, as property, acquired by law, ought not to be divested by any construction of the Constitution by implication; and that slavery in that instrument is not expressly abolished. It is true, without investigating the right of Christians to hold Africans in perpetual servitude, that they had been considered by some of the province laws as actually existing among us: but nowhere do we find it expressly established. It was a usage,—a usage which took its origins from the practice of some of the European nations and the regulations for the benefit of trade of the British government respecting its then colonies. But whatever usages formerly prevailed or slid in upon us by the example of others on the subject, they can no longer exist. Sentiments more favorable to the natural rights of mankind, and to that innate desire for liberty which heaven, without regard to complexion or shape, has planted in the human breast have prevailed since the glorious struggle for our rights began. And these sentiments led the framers of our constitution of government by which the people of this commonwealth have solemnly bound themselves to each other to declare—*that all men are born free and equal:* and that *every subject is entitled to liberty:* and to have it guarded by the laws as well as his life and property. In short, without resorting to implication in constructing the constitution, slavery is in my judgement as effectively abolished as it can be by the granting of rights and privileges wholly incompatible and repugnant to its existence. The court are therefore fully of the opinion that perpetual servitude can no longer be tolerated in our government, and that liberty can only be forfeited by some criminal conduct or relinquished by personal consent or contract . . . The Def[endan]t must be found guilty as the facts charged are not contraverted.

2.4.3

Excerpts from Justice William Atlee's decision in *Res publica v. Negro Betsey et al.*, Pennsylvania Supreme Court, 1789

The fifth section of the act requires entries of all the negro and mulatto slaves . . . it directs the mode of those entries; it fixes the time within which the entries shall be made; and, without any exception in respect to their ages, declares that no negro mulatto then within the State, should be deemed a slave or servant for life, . . . unless his or her name should be registered within the time limited. The master or owner had his election whether to enter them, or not; if he did, he secured himself the right he had in them before the making of the law; and, if he did not, it appears to have been the intention of the Legislature, that he should forfeit all right to their services. The tenth section, I think, shows this expressly; for, it not only enacts that such unregistered persons shall not be deemed as slaves, or servants for life . . . [but] that they shall be deemed, adjudged, and holden as free-men and free-women.

The full text of Document 2.4.3 is available on the CD-ROM.

2.4.4

Excerpts from judge's opinion in *Gobu v. Gobu*, Supreme Court of North Carolina, Hillsborough District, 1802

OPINION BY THE COURT. I acquiesce . . . to the presumption of every black person being a slave. It is so because the negroes originally brought to this country were slaves, and their descendants must continue slaves until manumitted by proper authority. If therefore a person of that description claims his freedom, he must establish his right to it by evidence as will destroy the force of the presumption arising from his color.

But I am not aware that the doctrine of presuming against liberty has been urged in relation to persons of mixed blood, or to those of any color between the two extremes of black and white; and I do not think it reasonable that such a doctrine should receive the least countenance. Such persons may have descended from Indians . . . at least in the maternal; mulatto parents originally free, in all which cases the offspring, following the condition of the mother, is entitled to freedom. Considering how many probabilities here are in favor of the liberty of these persons, they ought not to be deprived of it upon mere presumption, more especially as the right to hold them in slavery, if it exists, is in most instances, capable of being satisfactorily proved.

The full text of Document 2.4.4 is available on the CD-ROM.

2.4.5

Excerpts from the decision of Supreme Court of Appeals of Virginia in *Hudgins v. Wrights*, 1806

JUDGE TUCKER . . . From the first settlement of the colony of Virginia to the year 1778, (Oct. Sess) all Negroes, . . . brought into this country by sea, or by land, were slaves. And by the uniform declarations of our laws, the descendants of the females remain slaves to this day, unless they can prove a right to freedom, by actual emancipation, or by descent in the maternal line from an emancipated female.

. . . [A]ll American Indians brought into this country since the year 1705, and their descendants in the maternal line, are free . . . .

All white persons are and ever have been free in this country. If one evidently white, be notwithstanding claimed as a slave, the proof lies on the party claiming to make the other his slave.

The full text of Document 2.4.5 is available on the CD-ROM.

2.4.6

Excerpt from Chief Justic Parsons' decision in *Winchendon v. Hatfield*, 1808

Slavery was introduced into this country soon after its first settlement and was tolerated until the ratification of the present Constitution. The slave was the property of his master, subject to his orders and to reasonable correction for misbehavior, was transferable, like a chattel, by gift or sale, and was assets in the hands of his executor or administrator. If the master was guilty of cruel or unusual castigation of his slave, he was liable to be punished for the breach of the peace; and I believe the slave was allowed to demand sureties of the peace against a violent and barbarous master, which generally caused a sale to another master. And the issue of the female slave according to the maxim of the civil law, was the property of her master. Under these regulations the treatment of slaves was in general mild and humane, and they suffered hardships not greater than hired servants. Slaves were sometimes permitted to enjoy some privileges as *peculium*, with the profits of which they were enabled to purchase their manumission; and liberty was frequently granted to a faithful slave by the bounty of the master, sometimes in his life, but more commonly by his last will. Several negroes born in this country of imported slaves demanded their freedom of their masters by suit at law, and obtained it by a judgement of court. The defense of the master was faintly made for such was the temper of the times, that a restless, discontented slave was worth little; and when his freedom was obtained in a course of legal proceedings, the master was not holden for his future support if he became poor. But in the first action, involving the right of the master, which came before the Supreme Judicial Court, after the establishment of the constitution, the judges declared that by virtue of the first article of the Declaration of Rights, slavery in this State was no more.

The Life and Times of Elizabeth "Mum Bett" Freeman, 1742–1829

As the English colonies moved closer to the War of Independence, the intensity and pervasiveness of public discourse about the natural rights of human beings could not help but raise contradictions in the minds of many about a whole group of people being legally held in chattel bondage.

When Elizabeth Freeman came to work at the Ashley house in the 1740s, she was just a young girl and Sheffield was a frontier town in western Massachusetts. John Ashley was an up-and-coming businessman as well as a lawyer. Elizabeth, known then as Bet, and her little sister had been "given as wedding presents" to Mr. Ashley's young wife, Annetje, also called Hannah. The three of them probably spoke only Dutch when they came to Sheffield. Soldier, lawyer, and judge, John Ashley was well respected as a fair man in his community, but his wife was known to be demanding and capricious.

In an incident after almost thirty years of service, Mrs. Ashley tried to hit Elizabeth Freeman's sister, Lizzie, with a fire-heated hearth shovel and Freeman, now known as Mum Bett, stepped between them to receive the blow. The scar on her arm was visible for the rest of her life. More importantly, it was reported to be the motivation for Mum Bett to leave the Ashley home in the spring of 1781 and seek a lawyer to sue for her freedom from both Col. Ashley and his son, John Ashley Jr. Because he did not comply with Freeman's demand, Col. Ashley became the defendant in this case, and he was compelled to give up his twenty-year position as a popular local judge to avoid a conflict of interest.

Like the more famous Quok Walker case and many other freedom-from-slavery petitions that followed, Elizabeth Freeman and her lawyer, Theodore Sedgwick, based their claim on the Bill of Rights in the newly approved Massachusetts Constitution (1780), which stated that "all men are born free and equal" and that "every subject is entitled to liberty." Because she was a woman, Mum Bett had no legal standing in a court of law. She was, therefore, joined in her suit by Brom, an African American man who was also enslaved to the Ashley household. Despite an appeal to the Superior Court of Adjudicature, the Ashleys lost the case both there and in the lower Berkshire County Court of Common Pleas. The juries stated that Brom and

Bet had never been "the legal Negro servants" of the Ashleys, who were then required to pay damages of 30 shillings as well as the court costs of £5, 14 shillings and 4 pence.

Elizabeth Freeman went to work for her lawyer's family, the Sedgwicks, until she retired at an old age with savings, land, and many grandchildren. Her first husband had died fighting in the Revolutionary War. There is evidence that her second husband was an ancestor of W. E. B. Du Bois. Theodore Sedgwick, a close personal friend and a protege of John Ashley Sr., went on to become a delegate to the Continental Congress and Senator from Massachusetts.

Elizabeth "Mum Bett" Freeman's story is an especially powerful one because we have several anecdotal accounts of who she was as a person by people who knew and cared for her. In addition to court documents, we have her final will, which provides information about her relationship with the Sedgwicks and documents her belongings as well as some of her relatives. There is even a miniature watercolor painting of her likeness when she was an older woman. As with many early African Americans, we cannot read Elizabeth Freeman's actual words in her own writing, but unlike many, we can hear vivid details about the life she led and even her statements as they have been handed down by those who heard her speak them. As we read, it becomes clear that the stories share an antebellum northern white consciousness, revealing many levels of imbedded racism. Still, we are able to get some sense of what life was like for an African American woman in a northern community in the late eighteenth century.

Elizabeth Freeman lies buried in a Stockbridge, Massachusetts graveyard, apart, where people of color were put to rest. Her epitaph was written by the son of Judge Sedgwick, it reads:

> ELIZABETH FREEMAN,
> Known by the name of
> Mum Bett,
> Died December 28, 1829. Her supposed age was 85 years.
> She was born a slave, and remained a slave for nearly thirty years:
> she could neither read nor write, yet in her own sphere she
> had no superior nor equal: she neither wasted time or
> property: she never violated a trust, nor failed to
> perform a duty. In every situation of domestic
> trial, she was the most efficient helper
> and the tenderest friend.
> GOOD MOTHER, FAREWELL.

Organizing Idea

Expectations raised by the Revolution's rhetoric of liberty resulted in many African Americans petitioning the courts to seek their freedom. Elizabeth "Mum Bett" Freeman was one of those people. Her strength, competence, and self-respect positively affected all people who knew her.

LESSON 5: THE LIFE AND TIMES OF ELIZABETH "MUM BETT" FREEMAN

Student Objectives

Students will:

- learn to use primary and secondary source documents to piece together elements from one woman's life as they become familiar with a significant period in history and the historical figure Elizabeth Freeman
- gain some understanding of how court action can affect social practice
- make decisions about what kinds of information to include or leave out when creating a documentary portrait of someone's life

Key Questions

- What personal resources does it take to challenge a well-established economic and social institution?
- What conditions were present at the time of Elizabeth Freeman's case that made it possible for her to be successful?

Primary Source Materials

DOCUMENT 2.5.1: Elizabeth Freeman's watercolor portrait, 1811

DOCUMENT 2.5.2A AND B: Image and transcript of Elizabeth Freeman's last will and testament, October 8, 1829 (handwritten); image on CD only

DOCUMENTS 2.5.3: "Slavery in New England" by Catherine Maria Sedgwick, 1853

Supplementary Materials

ITEM 2.5.A: Additional vocabulary lists for primary sources
ITEM 2.5.B: Study guide for "Slavery in New England"

Student Activities

Reading and Discussion of the Will

Activity 1

As a class, examine the image of Elizabeth Freeman (2.5.1). Consider the name "Mum Bett," by which she was known. Can you tell anything about her? Now read the original copy of her will (2.5.2A), then read the transcript (2.5.2B). What do you notice about the way the document is written? What more can we learn about Elizabeth Freeman from the information that is provided in her will?

(Possible answers: handwritten, no periods, irregular capitalization, E. F. signs it with an X, indicating that she probably is unable to write; it includes parts that are crossed out, indicating that E. F. might have changed her mind about division of property as the will was being written; because designation of recipients and items jumps around a little, it is possible to envision the four women going from room to room inventorying the items as E. F. makes decisions about what to give to whom; we don't have information about who actually penned the document.)

Working individually or in small groups, ask students to find evidence to answer the following questions? State the documentation that provides evidence for the response and then give the answers.

- Did Elizabeth Freeman write this will herself? How do we know? Who was present with her as she inventoried her belongings and decided which items to give to whom? Why do you think Charles Sedgwick Jr. is not one of the witnesses?

- Did Elizabeth Freeman own any land and, if so, to whom does she bequeath it? How does she divide it and under what terms does she bequeath it? What does this tell us about her ability to plan for the future and the wisdom of her financial sense?

- To whom did Elizabeth Freeman leave the items listed in her will? Did Elizabeth Freeman have any descendents? If so, can we identify any individuals by name, as well as the number of generations? What might you speculate about Elizabeth Freeman's concern for her family? What can we say about her relationship with Charles Sedgwick Esq.?

- Given the descriptive details of some of the items that she leaves Josiah Amos and Lydia Maria, where do you think they lived at the time the will was written? Do we know how old they were?

- List at least eight items that you find identified in the will. Be sure to include a few that you think are the most valuable. What can you speculate about the nature of Elizabeth Freeman's economic status?

- Many people of African descent who lived in the eighteenth-century American colonies had arrived recently from Africa due to kidnapping from their villages and farms. Do you think that Elizabeth Freeman may have known her mother and father on this continent? What evidence do you have? Can we know for sure? Do we know the name they gave her as a baby in their arms?

Activity 2 Research Extension—Drawing Conclusions from a Will

Are any of the items of clothing or furniture in the will (2.5.2B) unfamiliar to you? Make a list. Find books at the library or information on the web that can help you explain their functions.

Given what you know about early American history, what do you think is the reason that Amos Josiah is left property but Lydia Maria does not receive any?

For more information about the kind of clothes Ms. Freeman was handing down, look at these websites:

African American women's clothing in eighteenth-century Virginia:
www.history.org/almanack/life/clothing/intro/african1.html

Women's clothing terms in eighteenth-century America:
www.history.org/almanack/life/clothing/women/index.html

Reading and Analyzing—"Slavery in New England" Activity 3

Through reading and discussion, students will explore Elizabeth Freeman's character and her influence on those around her, including nineteenth-century writer and feminist Catherine Maria Sedgwick. As a class, identify some of the qualities our culture associates with a "good" character or a "bad" character. On the board, brainstorm a list for each of these. Discuss what it means to "have a personality" and what is meant by "strength of character."

Divide students into groups of five. Distribute complete sets of "Slavery In New England" by Catherine Sedgwick (2.5.3) to each group. Ask a team member to be in charge of one section (note that Section 5 is shorter and may be of use to students with differing learning abilities). As a provocative guideline, ask students to try to identify places where they notice Sedgwick's genteel, and often not so subtle, racism.

- Each student should first answer the questions for the appropriate section on the Study Guide (Item 2.5.B).
- Then have students reread the section and make a list of the most important incidents from Mum Bett's life that Catherine Sedgwick chooses to describe. Next to each incident, students should write the personal qualities they believe Elizabeth Freeman demonstrates.
- Answers to the two section questions and the lists of characteristics can then be shared with the other group members. The small group can discuss these and see if there is agreement.
- Have each small group share their lists of personal qualities with the whole class.
- As a class, think about, discuss, and write down other things students wish they could find out about Mum Bett, things that they can now only guess at.

Essay Writing—Admirable Qualities Activity 4

Write a brief essay describing the qualities you most admire in Elizabeth Freeman. Be specific and give examples. Are there people in your own family or neighborhood who show the same kinds of personal qualities today? Close your essay by describing that person and some stories from his or her life.

Activity 5 — Reading "Slavery in New England" in Full

Students can read the complete article "Slavery in New England" (2.5.3) and answer these questions individually or in small groups:

- How does Sedgwick characterize the relationship between Mr. and Mrs. Ashley?
- What does she say about the "question of equality between the sexes"?
- What does she say was the cause of the pivotal shovel confrontation?
- How did Mum Bett help the "gal in trouble"?
- Did Mum Bett give the girl Mrs. Ashley's food?
- How did Elizabeth Freeman talk about freedom?
- What do you think Sedgwick means by "wider abuses make rebels?"
- Of the ways Mum Bett chose to resist the Shay's War men, which would you choose?
- Why do you think Mum Bett wasn't scared to die?
- This article was written in 1853 while chattel slavery was still legal in many states. How many years after Mum Bett won her freedom in court was it written? How many years after her death?

Activity 6 — Extended Research—Catherine Sedgwick

Catherine Sedgwick began to write in 1822, eight years before Mum Bett's death. Her work addressed issues of women's rights, prisons, slavery, and minority groups. Students can write a paper or create a detailed poster reflecting Sedgwick's work and her ideas.

Further Student and Teacher Resources

Chase, Arthur C. *The Ashleys: A Pioneer Berkshire Family*. Beverly, MA: The Trustees of the Reservations. (a very informative and comprehensive booklet)

Chronicles of Old Canaan, courtesy of the Sheffield Historical Society, page 22.

Cushing Family (William J.) Personal Papers, Massachusetts Historical Society, Boston, MA.

Earle, Alice Morse. *Home Life in Colonial Days*. New York: The MacMillan Co., 1898.

Eckert, Allen W. *The Frontiersmen*. New York: Little, Brown and Co., 1967.

Jones, Rhett S. "Trifling Patriots and a Freeborn People: Revolutionary Ideology and Afro-Americans." *Brown Alumni Monthly* 76 (December 1975): 23–28.

MacDonald, Mimi. "Mum Bett's Freedom Struggle," *The Berkshire Courier*, July 1981.

MacManus, Edgar J. *Black Bondage in the North.* Syracuse: Syracuse University Press, 1973.

Martineau, Harriet. "Restless Slaves," in *Report on Western Travels,* 1836.

Sedgwick, Theodore, and Catherine Maria Sedgwick. Personal Papers. Massachusetts Historical Society, Boston, MA.

Twombly, Robert. "Black Resistance to Slavery in Massachusetts." *Insights and Parallels: Problems and Issues of American Social History,* William O'Neill, ed. Minneapolis: Burgess Publishing, 1973.

Walter, Mildred Pitts. *Second Daughter: The Story of a Slave Girl.* New York: Scholastic Trade, 1996.

Wilds, Mary. *Mum Bett: The Life and Times of Elizabeth Freeman—The True Story of a Slave Who Won Her Freedom.* Greensboro, NC: Avisson Press, 1999.

Zilversmit, Arthur. "Mum Bett: Folklore and Fact." Taken from a speech given to the Berkshire Historical Society, 1969. Sheffield Family History Center, Sheffield, MA.

———. "Quok Walker, Mum Bett and the Abolition of Slavery in Massachusetts." *William & Mary Quarterly.* Volume XXV (1968).

Websites

www.MumBett.com

www.pbs.org/wgbh/aia/part2/2p39.html *Africans in America bio*

www.pbs.org/wgbh/aia/part2/2i1534.html *historian Margaret Washington's useful response to the question: "What's the significance of Elizabeth Freeman successfully suing for her freedom in Massachusetts?"*

www.thetrustees.org *select "westregion" for information on Colonel John Ashley's House, where Mum Bett worked as a slave. The house is open to the public.*

Catherine Sedgwick websites

www.bedfordstmartins.com/litlinks/fiction/sedgwick.htm

www.cohums.ohio-state.edu/english/People/Bracken.1/Sedgwick/

www.csustan.edu/english/reuben/pal/chap3/sedgwick.html

www.salemstate.edu/imc/sedgwick/index.html

www.earlyamerica.com/earlyamerica/notable/sedgwickc/index.html

www.theodoresedgwick.com/

Contemporary Connection

✣

A Notable American Woman

Although Elizabeth "Mum Bett" Freeman is not mentioned in the National Women's Hall of Fame, she is well known in Berkshire County, Massachusetts, and her story continues to be researched and documented by scholars. There is an official Mum Bett website: *http://MumBett.com*. The site offers viewers the opportunity to sign a letter petitioning to have a "Mum Bett" stamp and mentions an effort to transform the facts of her life into a TV series.

In the 1990s when two crisis centers for women merged in Berkshire County, the decision was made to rename the new agency as the Elizabeth Freeman Center. This name was chosen to honor a woman who found a way to rise above her situation—a woman who "stands in" to represent all women who struggle for a better life.

What are the names and stories of women in your community who have spoken up for their rights and whose actions have benefited others? Are there schools, community centers, or other institutions named after women? Students should research these questions and bring the information back to the class.

Primary Source Materials for Lesson 5

2.5.1

Elizabeth Freeman's watercolor portrait, 1811

Courtesy of Massachusetts Historical Society

2.5.2A AND B

Image and transcript of Elizabeth Freeman's last will and testament, October 8, 1829 (handwritten)

I Elizabeth Freeman of Stockbridge Massachusetts do make and publish this my last will and testament as follows—

1st after the payment of my past debts I hereby give & bequeath to Charles Sedgwick Esq. of Lenox all my real Estate (excepting that conveyed to my Great grandson Amos Josiah Van Schaac (sic)) in trust & for the uses & purposes herein after mentioned - that is to say It is my will & intention that one undivided half of said real Estate should be held by the said Charles for the sole use and benefit of my daughter Elizabeth & her heirs & the other half for the use & benefit of my Great Grandchildren Amos Josiah Van Schaack & Lydia Maria Ann Van Schaack & their heirs . . .

Secondly I give & bequeath my household furniture & other personal property as follows—To my Daughter Elizabeth I give the following articles viz:

Three gowns—1 black Silk—1 D°· ["ditto," an abbreviation that was often used to signify "that which is the same as what precedes it," i.e., another black silk gown] got from Philadelphia—1 D°· [black silk gown] recd of my father—my largest silk shawl—a large home made birds eye petticoat—a short gown that was my mothers a white shawl with flowers—2 linen pocket handkerchiefs—one marked B.

The image of Document 2.5.2A and the full text of Document 2.5.2B are available on the CD-ROM.

2.5.3

"Slavery in New England" by Catherine Maria Sedgwick, 1853

Mum-Bett's character was composed of few but strong elements. Action was the law of her nature, and conscious of superiority to all around her, she felt servitude intolerable. It was not the work—work was play to her. Her power of execution was marvellous. Nor was it awe of her kind master, or fear of her despotic mistress, but it was the galling of the harness, the irresistible longing for liberty. I have heard her say, with an emphatic shake of the head peculiar to her: "Any time, any time while I was a slave, if one minute's freedom had been offered to me, and I had been told I must die at the end of that minute, I would have taken it—just to stand one minute on God's *airth* a free woman—I would."

The full text of Document 2.5.3 is available on the CD-ROM.

LESSON 6

Using Government Records to Locate the African American Presence in Early American History

In 1656, Bostonian Ken was perhaps the first African American landowner in Massachusetts. He owned a house and a lot in Dorchester as well as four acres of land that were planted in wheat.

Lucy Terry Prince of Deerfield, Massachusetts, lived from 1724 to 1821 and was one of the first American women of any ethnicity whose poetry has been recorded. Certain events in her life, such as arguing before the trustees of Williams College and the United States Circuit Court in Vermont, are based more on tradition than documentation. However, records affirm that she was a remarkable woman, known for her eloquence and as a champion for justice.

Born in 1785, Rhode Island's Eleanor Eldridge ran a successful painting and wallpapering business during the early 1800s, which enabled her to build her own house on a lot in Providence.

These are some early African Americans, who are probably unknown to us because the stories of their lives have not been included in the history books. However, as more archival material is closely searched for records, the vivid fabric of these multifaceted lives begins to emerge to reveal a fascinating panorama.

The new U.S. government authorized the first census in 1790. It listed "Free white males of 16 years and upward, including heads of families," "Free white males under 16 years," "Free white females, including heads of families," "all other persons," and "slaves." These "other persons" were most likely free people of color in the early days after the American Revolution. (Because most Native American people were not taxed, the government chose to exclude them from the census rolls.) Using the census, it is possible to look in almost any town in a northern state listed and immediately identify one, two, or more households of color, probably African American. Unfortunately, the census records contain numerous gaps and errors. There are hundreds of examples of individuals whose names appear on soldier muster rolls, probate records, or elsewhere but who fail to show up in the national census.

Who were the "other persons" listed in the census? What sort of record did these African American individuals and families leave behind them? Is it possible to uncover the stories of people who have been ignored in our history books?

Once a researcher has identified a name, he or she can begin searching the multitude of local, state, and federal records that document ordinary events, leaving traces of daily life. These records include marriages, births, deaths, wills, property deeds, receipts, court cases, and newspaper announcements.

Research at the local level may uncover the presence of other African Americans. It's like a mystery novel. One discovery leads to another and can take you in whole new directions. The activities in this lesson create a research experience for the student.

Organizing Idea

Research can bring into the foreground African American stories that have gone untold. Through researching public records, students and teachers can find local connections to African American history.

Student Objectives

Students will:

- learn some of the many ways in which federal, state, and local agencies keep records through which we can learn about peoples' lives
- learn strategies to identify and research individual African American people in particular communities
- explore African American names common in colonial America and the early national period

Key Questions

- What evidence is left in records after people die? How did individual African Americans make their living? What were their communities like? Who was in their communities? Did people stay in one place? Were pensioners entitled to veterans' benefits able to collect what they were promised? Did African American pensioners receive different treatment?
- Why does the federal government take a census? How accurate are population records and what may cause errors? What others kinds of public records are kept at the state and local levels?
- How did people who couldn't read and write create letters and legal documents?

Primary Source Materials

DOCUMENT 2.6.1: Excerpt from "List of Free Black Heads of Families in the First Census of the United States, 1790"

DOCUMENT 2.6.2: Excerpt from "List of Black Servicemen Compiled from the War Department Collection of Revolutionary War Records"

DOCUMENT 2.6.3: "A Schedule of the Ancient Colored Inhabitants, of Charlestown, Mass., on record prior to 1800" compiled on January 1, 1870

DOCUMENT 2.6.4: Deposition of Prince Robinson, March 9, 1815

DOCUMENT 2.6.5: Deposition of Prince Robinson, April 10, 1819

DOCUMENT 2.6.6: Duplicate certificate for Prince Robinson, April 23, 1819

DOCUMENT 2.6.7: Deposition of Ann, wife of Prince Robinson, January 21, 1840

DOCUMENT 2.6.8: Deposition of Charlotte T. Tumber, January 18, 1837

DOCUMENT 2.6.9: Deposition of Jabez Proctor, Cavendish, Vermont, September 16, 1837

DOCUMENT 2.6.10: Deposition of Jesse Gove, January 23, 1840

Supplementary Materials

ITEM 2.6.B: Guide to origins of African American names

ITEM 2.6.C: Answer key for "A Schedule of the Ancient Colored Inhabitants"

ITEM 2.6.D: A Guide to Using Public Records

Vocabulary

affidavit	depose and	head of household	status
census	testify	pension	transcript
cross-reference	genealogy	solemn oath	warned (out)

Student Activities

Common African American Names

Activity 1

Students should skim through the two lists from the National Archives (2.6.1 and 2.6.2). Then they should read the information on the possible sources of African American names (Item 2.6.B). Have students return to the documents and try to identify names of African derivation, place names, classical names, and names that might indicate status as free people. Find at least seven for each category and place them under the appropriate heading. Some of the names do not fall into any of the categories. Where do you think they might have originated?

Seeking the Details in Public Records

Activity 2

The purpose of this activity is to explore the kinds of information that can be found in a simple list of records, such as Documents 2.6.1 and 2.6.2. How do we know if the information is accurate? Is there any way to cross-reference? What other kinds of questions are we led to ask? Read through the entire list of 178 entries. What kinds of impressions do you get? Take notes if you want. Then answer these questions:

1. What life events are recorded in this list?
2. What sources of information are cited?
3. Can you find the person who owned a home?
   a. During which years (approximately) did the person live?
   b. What kind of work did he do?
   c. What was the location of his house?
4. Identify at least five entries that document African Americans who were not enslaved or who had achieved a "free" status. Write down these names and anything else you can know about them.
5. Identify at least five different ways by which the entries indicate that the institution of slavery existed in Charlestown.
6. List five people who had names with African roots, and write down anything else you learn about each of them.
7. List the number of entries that record people who had "classical" names, common at that time for African American people.
8. List the number of entries that record people who had "location," or "geographic," names, also common at that time for African American people. What other ways are there to identify an African American presence in a community?

Note: Item 2.6.C provides an answer key. It is available on the CD-ROM.

Activity 3 — Writing Extension—Assessing Accuracy

Pick one of the entries on the list and think about the questions we asked at the start. Write your answers to the following questions:

- ❖ What leads you to believe the information that is recorded in the chosen entry is accurate, and is there any way to know for sure? For example, the entry may include a classical name and, because this was common for African American people in Massachusetts at that time, it lends credence to the entry.
- ❖ One way to support the accuracy would be to find other mention of both the event recorded and/or any of the names involved. For what sources of information or documentation would you look to cross-reference the entry? Be as specific as possible and list as many as you can think of, such as town records and church or parish records that list marriages and baptisms.
- ❖ What other kinds of questions does the chosen entry make you curious about? What else would you like to know about the person or the event that is recorded here?

Finally, write at least a paragraph about any thoughts or feelings that come to you after you have completed this activity.

Examining Documents—Piecing Together the Robinsons' Life

Activity 4

All that we know about the lives of Ann and Prince Robinson comes from the 1790 U.S. Census and documents that are part of the Revolutionary War Pension and Bounty Land Warrant Applications, accessible at any regional National Archive center, free and open to the public.

Divide the class into small groups and give a set of all the documents (2.6.4–2.6.10) to each group. Students should examine these carefully to see how much they can learn about this African American couple who lived two hundred years ago. Provide each group a complete list of questions. Each group should answer the questions they can from the information contained in their documents.

- How many children did Prince and Ann have, what were their names, and what was their gender?
- Where did they meet? Where and when did they get married and by whom?
- What was the relationship between Jesse Gove and the Robinson family?
- What kind of work did the eldest Robinson child do and for whom did she work?
- What kind of work did Ann Robinson do at one point?
- Where did Prince Robinson and Peter Tumber come from originally?
- Which of them owned land and stock and how much?
- What were the names of Peter Tumber's wife and daughter?
- How large a pension was Prince Robinson receiving and why did he stop collecting? What remedy was he seeking from the government?
- Did Prince Robinson get what he wanted from the government records office?
- What injuries did Prince Robinson sustain and how did it affect him?
- How was Prince Robinson rescued from the battlefield?
- Could Ann and/or Prince Robinson read or write? On what do you base your answer?
- Was Prince Robinson a free person or an enslaved person? On what information do you base your answer?
- How did Peter Tumber become a free person?
- Is there any other information you found out that you would like to add?

Discuss these questions as a class:

- How does Ann build her case? What tools of persuasion does she use to convince the War Department that her claim to a widow's pension is justified?
- What was the final outcome of Ann Robinson's petition? What reason did they offer to justify their decision? Do you agree with their decision? Why or why not?

Activity 5   **Individual Reflection in Writing—How Did These Documents Contribute to Your Knowledge?**

Using examples from Documents 2.6.4–2.6.10, write your answers to these questions:

- ❖ Name three things you learned about early America that you didn't know before.
- ❖ What one or two facts do you think most effectively prove that Prince Robinson was a veteran of the Revolutionary War and why?
- ❖ Did anything surprise you?
- ❖ Is there any way that your conception of early America has shifted after doing this activity? If it did, how? If it didn't, what ideas or understandings were reinforced?

Activity 6   **Extended Research Using Public Records**

Item 2.6.D, "A Guide to Using Public Records," gives teachers and students detailed information on the resources available to conduct primary source research. For an advanced research project, students can identify individuals in their community, perhaps ancestors, and use public records to recreate their lives.

Further Students and Teacher Resources

Boles, John B. *Black Southerners, 1619–1869*. Lexington: University Press of Kentucky, 1984.

Higginbotham, A. Leon Jr. *In the Matter of Color—Race and the American Legal Process: The Colonial Period*. New York: Oxford University Press, 1980.

Johnson, Anne E., and Adam M. Cooper. *A Student's Guide to African American Genealogy—Oryx American Family Tree Series*. Phoenix, AZ: Oryx Press, 1986. (contains an extensive early African and African American history and modern culture bibliography)

Kaplan, Sidney, ed. *The Black Presence in the Era of the American Revolution, 1770–1800*. Greenwich, CT: New York Graphic Society, 1973.

Newman, Debra L., compiler. *Black History: A Guide to Civilian Records in the National Archives*. Published by the National Archives and Records Administration, 1984.

Piersen, William D. *Black Yankees: The Development of Afro-American Subculture in Eighteenth-Century New England*. Amherst, MA: University of Massachusetts Press, 1988.

Websites

Note: For researching U.S. census records, start with the website of the U.S. National Archives and Records Administration (NARA). The address for African American records is:

www.archives.gov/research_room/genealogy/research_topics/african_american_research.html

Each regional National Archives facility has a web page, accessible from **www.nara.gov/regional** including genealogical records and microfilm.

The Web version of the Guide to Federal Records in the National Archives of the United States **www.nara.gov/guide/** *(also: www.archives.gov as of 12/2001)* offers a portal to a huge amount of other resources.

The Digital Classroom—Primary sources, activities and training for educators and students, **www.nara.gov/education/classrm.html,** encourages teachers of students at all levels to use archival documents in the classroom. The Digital Classroom provides materials from the National Archives, methods for teaching with primary sources, and information on the most recent census.

Contemporary Connection

Discovering Information

Additional information on the experiences of African American life can be found at the Schomburg Center for Research in Black Culture, *www.nypl.org/research/sc,* a branch of the New York Public Library. In 1926, the personal collection of African American scholar and bibliophile Arturo Alfonso Schomburg was added to the Division of Negro Literature, History and Prints of The New York Public Library. Schomburg acted as curator until his death, when the center was renamed in his honor. This specialized museum provides insights into many aspects of African American culture from colonial times and before to the present day. The collections include art and artifacts, videotapes, books, manuscripts, periodicals, photographs, prints, online exhibits, recorded music discs, and sheet music, all related to different aspects of black culture. Another specialized museum is the Smithsonian's Anacostia Museum and Center for African American History and Culture, located at *www.si.edu/anacostia/.* After searching the web using the sites listed with this lesson, students can identify which sites were best, for example, which offered the most information, and which were truly user friendly. Students can consider creating their own class website for other students to use.

Primary Source Materials for Lesson 6

2.6.1

Excerpt from "List of Free Black Heads of Families in the First Census of the United States, 1790"

From Connecticut:

Name	Number in Family
Dimon, Nimrod	4
Dina (Negro)	1
Dinah (Negro)	2
Dinah (Negro)	1
Domine (Negro)	3
Doras (Negro)	2
Duplax	5
Easter (Negro)	3
Edward (Negro)	6
Edwards, Cuff	4
Eli (Negro)	6
Elie	1
Eran (Negro)	2
Fagins (Negro)	5
Fassion (Negro)	3
Fitch, Cuff (Negro)	9
Finch, Stephen	6
Florah (Negro)	2
Frank (Negro)	6
Frank, Robin	7
Freedom, Jack	4
Freeman (Negro)	4
Freeman, Call	4
Freeman, Cato	4

The full text of Document 2.6.1 is available on the CD-ROM.

2.6.2

Excerpt from "List of Black Servicemen Compiled from the War Department Collection of Revolutionary War Records"

Continental Troops:

Name	Regiment	Rank	Roll No.	Card No.
Cato, George	Grayson	Pvt.	9	1796
Ceasar, Bay		Pvt.	3	11
Ceasar, Solomon	Sherburne	Pvt.	9	2250
Cesar	Misc.		9	2414
Congo, Jack		Pvt.	11	2994
Cuff, James	Henley	Pvt.	12	6300
Erises, Sippo	Warner	Pvt.	17	4002
Flemming, Cato	16	Pvt.		5026
Free, John	Malcom	Pvt.		3860
Freeman, Prince	Sherburne	Pvt.		4013
Hanlen, Africa	23	Cpl.	22	6592
Heard, Ceasar	Misc.	Waiter	24	1618
Hunn, William (Negro)	Quartermaster	Wagoner	26	5251
Johnson, Cato	Spencer	Pvt.	27	5737
Martin, Ceasar	Misc.		33	4460
Mumford, Cato	Hazen	Pvt.	37	4101
Negro, Adam	Warnet	Pvt.	38	462
Negro, Stephen	2	Pvt.	38	512
Negroe, Cezar	4		38	521

The full text of Document 2.6.2 is available on the CD-ROM.

2.6.3A AND B

"A Schedule of the Ancient Colored Inhabitants, of Charlestown, Mass., on record prior to 1800" compiled on January 1, 1870

According to the original newspaper notice in the Charlestown Chronicle *of Massachusetts, Climax Excelsior compiled this "accurate account" on the seventh anniversary of "Mr. Lincoln's immortal proclamation of emancipation." We don't know why the list was reprinted into a little pamphlet or by whom. On the document, the words "By [Harrold Edes]" are handwritten.*

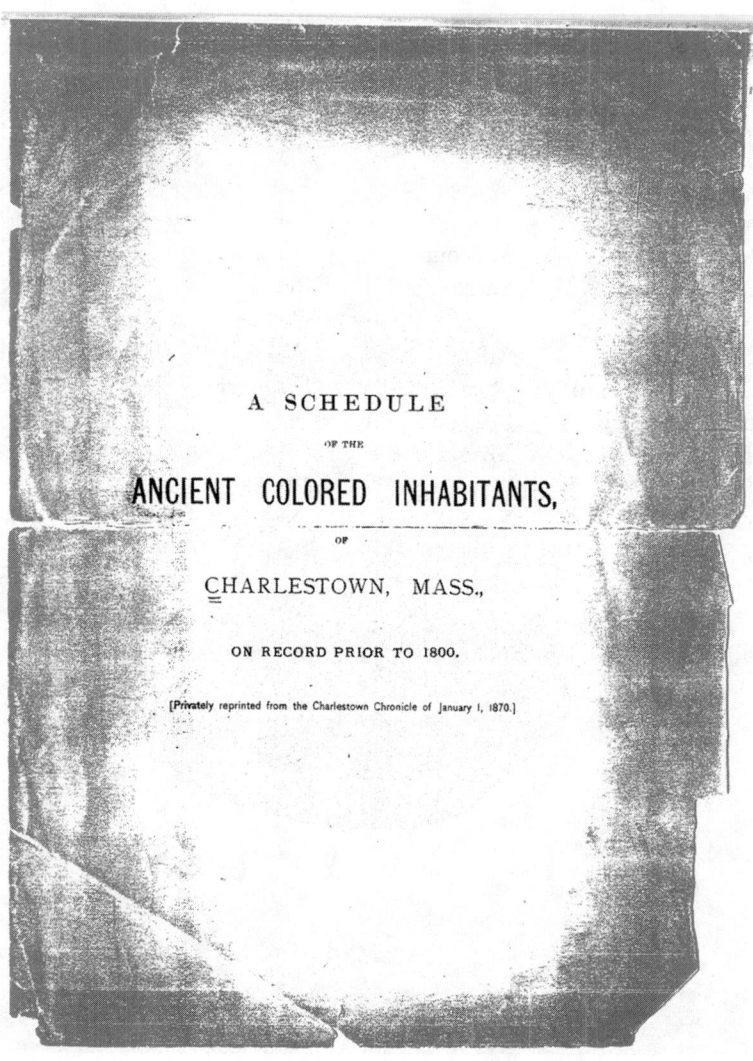

A Schedule of the Ancient Colored Inhabitants.

1. Adam; belonged to E. Cheever, died about 1740.
2. Bacchus; servant of Capt. Douse, married to Bilhah, Dec. 9, 1771.
3. Bacchus Biscom; d. March 21, 1785.
4. Bandon; of R. Temple, d. aged 80, October 14, 1792.
5. Blackwell; of S. Dowse, d. a. 70, 1746.
6. Boston; m. to Cimbo, servants of T. Lynde, May 4, 1741.
7. Boston; a. 80, aided by State, 1780. From Mass. Archives, vol. 141:379.
8. Cambridge; of B. Bunker, d. March 1, 1712-13.
9. Canongo; sold by N. Trerice to E. Johnson, 1693.
10. Cato Seeres and Mary Mingo, m. Oct. 28, 1700.
11. Cato; given, by John Miller's will, to Sarah Russell, 1767.
12. Cato; N. Frothingham's negro, in jail, Dec. 1770.
13. Cato; in E. Sheaf's Adm. Acct., 1771.
14. Cesar; of E. Austin, d. Dec. 29, 1721.
15. Cesar and wife Ann had
16. Cesar and Pompey baptized May 3, 1724, from church record.
17. Cesar; servant of J. Marshall, 1730.
18. Cesar; bought at age of 22 by T. Symmes, a. 1740 (?).
19. Cesar; servant of Mr. Trumbull, on his own account, bap. March 22, 1741.
20. Cesar; servant of Thomas Call, also on his own account, bap. March 22, 1741.
21. Cesar; in Boston 7 months, warned, March 31, 1755.
22. Cesar; of Eben Brooks, of Medford, and Zipporah, m. June 5, 1757.
23. Charles Dungeon and Maudlin Ward, m. Feb. 26, 1708, 2d m. to Phillis, Sept. 16, 1728.
24. Charlestown; of R. Luist, bap. Dec. 24, 1749; the same (?) warned at Boston, March 31, 1755; the same (?) servant of T. Flucker, published in Boston to Violet, servant of S. Whitwell, Dec. 10, 1761.
25. Cromwell; free, and Grace, m. Oct. 6, 1748.
26. Cuffee and Jenny; servants to Captain Wyer, m. Nov. 14, 1734.
27. Devonshire; d Dec. 7. 1721.
28. Ephraim; left by W. Wyer, 1748.
29. Fortune; a. 22, in B. Gerrish's inv. July 31, 1750; belonged to H. Gowen's estate, 1762.
30. Geoffrey, brother of J. Anthony, with C. Chambers, 1744.
31. Gloucester; of J. Marshall 1730.
32. Hereford; of D. Russell, d. of s. px. 1721.
33. Ishmael; of Lincoln and Zilpha, born 1731, bap. Jan. 30, 1731-2.
34. Israel; from Malden, warned 1757.
35. Jack and wife, Claris; of Capt. C. Chambers; bought freedom, June 13, 1706, per Inferior Court files.
36. Jack and Jane; m, August 21, 1729.
37. Jack; of Mrs. Parker, and Flora, m. Dec. 16, 1742.

Courtesy of Bienecke Library, Yale University

The full text of Document 2.6.3 is available on the CD-ROM.

2.6.4

Deposition of Prince Robinson, March 9, 1815

State of Vermont
Rutland County

This may certify that Prince Robinson A Negro Man Personally appeared before me Nathan Osgood [?] one of the Justices of the Peace within and for the County of Rutland and made solemn oath that he is the same Prince Robinson a Negro who received actual wounds during the Revolutionary War, that he was then a private in Capt. John Waits Company in Colonel Green's Regiment—and was placed upon the pension list in the year 1802 —

In Witness whereof I have herunto [led?] my hand at Rutland in the County of Rutland this 9th day of March Anno Domini 1815.

Nathan Osgood Just. Peace

2.6.5

Deposition of Prince Robinson, April 10, 1819

State of Vermont

Rutland County } Be it known the before me William Page one of the Justices of the Peace in the County aforesaid on the tenth day of April 1819, Personally appeared Prince Robinson a Negro and made solemn oath that he is the identical Prince Robinson who received actual wounds during the Revolutionary War, that he was a Private in Capt. John Waits Company in Col. Green's Regiment, that he was placed on the pensions list , Roll of Vermont Agency in the year 1802 at a full pension, that he is now entitled to pension of eight dollars per month on account of his wounds received during the Revolutionary War.

The full text of Document 2.6.5 is available on the CD-ROM.

2.6.6

Duplicate certificate for Prince Robinson, April 23, 1819

Duplicate

___**Vermont**___

Prince Robinson
   Private
Capt Wait's Co & Col.
Greens reg. in the Army
U.S. during the Revolutionary
War. _____
_____
_____

Ration of distb — Total
_____

Inscribed on the roll of
Vermont at $5 per mo:
To commence 1 Jan.y
1803 _ Increased to $8. _
per mo: by Law of 24
of April, 1816. _____

_____

_____

Duplicate certificate
of pension issued 23.d of
April 1819 and sent
to the pensioner care of
James Cheney Esq. Rutland
Vermont _____

_____

_____

<u>2.6.7</u>

Deposition of Ann, wife of Prince Robinson, January 21, 1840

State of Vermont]
    Rutland County [Js?] On this twenty-first day of January, 1840, Ann Robinson, aged 100 years and upwards, personally appeared before the Hon.r William Hall, Judge of the Probate Court of Rutland Vermont . . . [She] doth make the following declaration in order to obtain the benefit of the provision made by the act of Congress, passed July 4, 1836.
    That she is the widow of Prince Robinson, who was a private in the American Army, of the Revolution, and served in that capacity till the close of the war; during a part of which service, and she doth not know how much of it, he was a private in Capt. John Wait's Company in Colonel Greens Regiment, commonly called the Black Regiment, which Regiment, after it was cut up and nearly destroyed at Crumpond, was transferred into a White Regiment, at that time commanded by a Colonel Olney, of Rhode Island, as she hath been informed. That the said Prince Robinson was a pensioner of the United States, at the rate of 96 dollars a year: and for proofs of his serving she hereby refers to the declaration and vouchers of the said Prince Robinson and the Rolls of the said Black Regiment, and other military records now in the war office of the United States.

The full text of Document 2.6.7 is available on the CD-ROM.

2.6.8

Deposition of Charlotte T. Tumber, January 18, 1837

I, Charlotte T. Tumber of Cavendish in the County of Windsor and State of Vermont, aged thirty three years on the 18th day of January, 1837, do depose and testify and say that I am the youngest daughter of Peter Tumber, and Phillis Tumber, deceased. That I have known and been acquainted for many years with Prince Robinson, a black man, late of Rutland in the County of Rutland in said state of Vermont, deceased, and with his wife, now his widow, Anna Robinson, now living in said Rutland . . . .

I have heared (sic) my father tell a great deal about a W. Clark, Justice of the Peace, who was said to have married Prince and Anna; that he knew W. Clark. I have often heared both Prince and Ann tell the same story, that they were married while Prince was in the army, by the same Justice of the Peace, W. Clark. I have many times, heared a great deal more, from both of them, about their services in the war.

The full text of Document 2.6.8 is available on the CD-ROM.

2.6.9

Deposition of Jabez Proctor, Cavendish, Vermont, September 16, 1837

I, Jabez Proctor, of Cavendish in the County of Windsor and State of Vermont aged fifty seven years do depose testify and say that I was acquainted with Peter Tumber for about forty years previous to his death, which took place five or six years ago, and that he was during said period a resident of Cavendish aforesaid, his general reputation for truth and sincerity was good. His uniform moral character was considered good, and he was not reputed as being in the habit of embellishing stories, I have understood from him, and I should think from others, that he was a soldier in the American Army of the Revolutionary War.

The full text of Document 2.6.9 is available on the CD-ROM.

2.6.10

Deposition of Jesse Gove, January 23, 1840

I, Jesse Gove, of Rutland, Vermont, aged 55, do depose, testify and say that I have known Prince Robinson and his wife, Ann, ever since they came to reside in this town in the spring or summer season of 1795. In the spring of 1796 they went into and occupied, by my father's permission, a small back tenement on his premises, where they remained through that summer, and perhaps longer—how long, I do not recollect . . . .

Prince, since my knowledge of him, was lame in one of his lower limbs and blind in one eye, both proceeding from wounds as he stated he received while in the service of the United States at the time of the Black Regiment was cut to pieces in battle in the revolutionary war, and to which Regiment Prince claimed to have belonged. I have several times heard Jacob Lawyer, a late pensioner but now deceased relate many of the circumstances relative to Prince's being wounded. Lawyer was a white man, and in the service at the same time; and, as he stated, was one of the party and the identical man who, after the discomfiture of the said regiment, took Prince "in his arms" from among the dead and wounded on the field and carried him into camp.

The full text of Document 2.6.10 is available on the CD-ROM.

LESSON 7

African Americans in the Whaling Industry

In the early 1800s, free African American men were about seven times more likely to go to sea than men of European descent. In his book *Black Jacks: African Americans in the Age of Sail,* Jeffrey Bolster writes that in 1819 and 1820, African American men comprised 18.4 percent of the crews shipping out of Philadelphia, 17.4 percent in New York, and 23 percent in Providence, Rhode Island (pp. 235–77). This was consistent with a legacy of maritime work that began along the rivers and coasts of Africa. It continued when enslaved Africans were employed as seamen, ship officers, and sometimes even captains on coastal merchant and fishing vessels.

A seaman's life offered an African American opportunities. If he were enslaved and his earnings went to his owner, life at sea nevertheless brought a slave into increased contact with African Americans, free and enslaved. In ports where the vessel docked, he was exposed to ideas and alternative cultures and traditions. There were more opportunities to run away successfully. For a free black man, the maritime industry was one of few where he could earn wages close to those earned by European Americans. Black seamen, free or enslaved, became part of a large national and international network.

Discrimination existed on board ship, but a black seaman was more likely to be judged by his skills than the color of his skin. When a storm hit, a man's race became irrelevant. It mattered that he could reef a sail, throw a line to a sailor swept overboard, or remain calm at the helm. "This reality is what earned blacks respect or at least they were tolerated, even though they were not always accepted," writes Patricia McKissack in *Black Hands, White Sails: The Story of African-American Whalers* (p. 16).

Whaling, in particular, allowed African Americans to be in the mainstream of an industry. The hunting of whales dates back over two thousands years to the Inuit people. It continued when Native Americans and European colonists cut up beached whales or killed ones swimming in coastal waters. By the late 1700s, few whales could be found close to shore, and deep-sea whale hunting began to emerge as a major industry. Over the next century, whale ships would exhaust the supply of the giant mammals in the Atlantic and take even longer and more dangerous voyages to the Arctic and the Pacific. Nantucket Island and later New Bedford, Massachusetts, became the whaling capitals of the world.

Why venture so far in search of whales? Ship owners stood to make huge profits. Whales were the source of oil that, when converted into fuel for lamps, burned cleaner and longer than oil from other sources. Whale oil was also used for soap, smokeless candles, and lubricants. Other parts of the whale could be used for bristles in brushes and brooms, and the bones were made into umbrella frames and ladies' corsets. The most valuable product was ambergris, a substance only rarely found in the intestinal bile of a whale and used for perfume.

The life of seamen has always been fraught with danger, but the life of a whaler was exceptionally so. Voyages of two to three years were the norm; many stretched to four years. The process of killing a 50-foot sperm whale from a 30-foot whale boat was difficult and hazardous. And when the crew finally towed the dead whale and tied it up alongside the whale ship, the foul-smelling, bloody, greasy, and exhausting work began. Men cut up the carcass and boiled the blubber to extract the oil in the ship's try-works, huge iron pots set in brick ovens. If any man ventured on a whaling voyage with romantic notions, these were quickly dispelled by his first encounter with a whale.

Why did so many African Americans sail on whaling vessels? It was one of the few opportunities they had to be paid according to their skill and to rise in the ranks based on achievement. Quakers owned many whale ships. Most opposed slavery, and they were more open to employing African Americans. A whaler shared in the risks of the voyage, but he also shared in the profits, earning a small, agreed-upon share called a "lay."

The discovery of oil in Pennsylvania in 1859 and the loss of scores of whaling vessels during the Civil War spelled the beginning of the end of the whaling industry. However, even as the number of whaling vessels declined, the percentage of men of color manning them increased. African Americans were increasingly excluded from merchant vessels but not whale ships. Also, white men were more likely to work in the growing number of factories and mills. By the late 1870s, men of color comprised more than half of the whaling crews. Whaling vessels, though fewer in number, needed labor, and black men supplied it.

Organizing Idea

African American mariners contributed greatly to the growth of the whaling industry through their strength, perseverance, and skills. Whaling provided an economic base and communications network for African American sailors in the eighteenth and nineteenth centuries.

Student Objectives

Students will:

- ❖ learn some of the stories of African American mariners
- ❖ understand how whaling offered the African American community an opportunity to build an economic base, even though the work meant long absences from family

❖ begin to understand some of the ramifications of the Negro Seaman's Act of 1822

Key Questions

❖ What kinds of opportunities did whaling present, and how did African Americans use them to their advantage?

❖ What types of jobs did the whaling industry provide?

❖ What risks did African American mariners face?

Primary Source Materials

DOCUMENT 2.7.1: Portrait of Absalom Boston

DOCUMENT 2.7.2: Inventory and appraisal of Absalom F. Boston's estate, 1855

DOCUMENT 2.7.3: Selected stanzas of the 72-verse song "Ballad of the Industry," about the 1822 whaling voyage

DOCUMENT 2.7.4: Painting of whaleman about to harpoon a whale, 1835

DOCUMENT 2.7.5: Image of the crew list of the whaling brig *Elizabeth*, 1841

Supplementary Materials

ITEM 2.7.A: Additional vocabulary lists for primary sources

ITEM 2.7.B: Chart for the crew of the *Milton* with each man's lay

ITEM 2.7.C: Answer key calculating each crew member's lay

Vocabulary

apprentice	coastal	greenhand	schooner
bark	cooper	harpooner	ship's steward
boatsteerer	deepsea	inventory	try-works
bootblacker	estate	lay	whale boat
brig	foc's'cle	merit-based	whaler

Student Activities

Activity 1 — Discovering Absalom Boston

Absalom Boston (1785–1855) was the only known black whaling captain on Nantucket Island, Massachusetts. Students should examine his portrait (2.7.1) and read the inventory of his estate taken after his death (2.7.2).

❖ Were many people able to afford a portrait?

❖ What can you learn about Absalom Boston by looking at his portrait?

- A dollar in 1855 was worth approximately $20 today. How large was Boston's estate?
- What do you learn about Absalom Boston from the inventory of his estate? What else would you like to know and where can you find answers?

Students may be interested in researching the case of Absalom Boston's uncle, Prince Boston, who in 1769 sailed out of Nantucket a slave but, following litigation, received the wages for his work and gained his freedom. In 1845, Absalom Boston also sought justice in the courts; he was one of the litigants seeking access for black children to the Nantucket's public schools.

Analyzing the *Industry's* Song

Activity 2

The ballad song (2.7.3) is best read aloud. What do you learn about the voyage and the crew? What is meant by "We dropt our boats got fast to one"? Students should look at the image of a whaleboat pursuing a whale (2.7.4) to help them picture the scene. What is the spirit of the song?

African Americans on Whaling Voyages

Activity 3

Look carefully at the image of the whaleboat approaching the whale (2.7.4).

- Who is in the boat?
- What are they doing?
- What does this show you about whaling?
- What questions do you have and where can you find answers?

Now examine the crew list for the *Elizabeth* (2.7.5).

- How many members of the crew appear to be of African descent?
- What's the range in age of crew members?
- How many are of Captain Cook's age or younger?
- Where is the *Elizabeth* headed? Why isn't the destination more specific?
- What questions do you have after examining this document? Where can you find answers?

Calculating—How Much Did They Earn?

Activity 4

This activity encourages students to think about the types of jobs on a whale ship, the changing nature of wages and money values, and the difference in value, or "stratification," given to jobs aboard ship. It also gives students a sense of how much money people actually earned in the first half of the nineteenth century.

In 1836, the net profit after expenses for the whale ship *Milton* was $99,994. It was normal for the owners of a ship to receive between 60 percent and 70 percent of the profits and the rest to be divided among the crew. Using the chart included on the CD-ROM (Item 2.7.B), first define each job and how much the men working at each job made for a two-year trip. Then calculate how much they were making per month, week, and hour. Finally, calculate approximately what those amounts would be worth today. This task could be a group project, with individual students choosing only one or two job descriptions to calculate and then compiling the information with others. (*Note:* $1 in 1836 is worth approximately $14 today.) An answer key (Item 2.7.C) is available on the CD-ROM.

Activity 5 **Further Research on African American Mariners**

Students can choose one of many African American seamen whose stories are at least partially recorded. They can write papers or create detailed collages to reflect the life of the person they pick. The class can display their findings as an exhibit for the school community. Possible choices include: John Mashow or Lewis Temple of New Bedford, Massachusetts; Nancy Gardner Prince and her husband, Nero Prince, originally of Newburyport, Massachusetts; Pardon Cook of Massachusetts; Standley Battou of Oxford, Maryland; Jude Hall of Exeter, New Hampshire; Ben Leggs of Virginia; and Paul Cuffe of Westport, Massachusetts.

Activity 6 **Writing Extension—Do I Help the Fugitive Slave?**

In 1847, enslaved oysterman Joshua Davis from Portsmouth, Virginia, was successfully stowed away on a boat and brought to freedom in Boston, via New York. In 1858, Tom Wilson was brought on board the cotton ship *Metropolis* and hidden among the bales by some of the "coloured crew" while it was docked in New Orleans, Louisiana. Later his presence was betrayed by "one of the colored men," but the searchers weren't able to find the stowaway. That same year, free African American William Brodie, of the bark *Overman* out of New York, was sentenced to be "sold for sixty-five years" for helping slaves to freedom in Darien, Georgia.

Have students imagine that they are the second mate on the whaling ship *John Adams* out of Nantucket, Massachusetts. They are returning from the whale hunting grounds off the coast of southern Africa in 1829. The *John Adams* has docked in Wilmington, Delaware, to pick up fresh food supplies and to exchange several thousand pounds of baleen for corn to sell when they head home further north. It has come to their attention that a person escaping from slavery on a small farm outside Baltimore, Maryland, has been secretly brought on board by the cook. A local sheriff has come on board asking if they have any information.

In most southern states, a person can be jailed for up to ten years if he or she is found to have withheld information or aided a runaway. In Georgia, a person can be sold into slavery if he or she is African American. In North Carolina, death is the potential penalty for helping a person escape. If seamen report what they know, the hidden man will certainly, at the very least, be returned to his owner. At worst, he will also be severely beaten and perhaps even maimed for life, sold away from his family, or sold to the plantations in the West Indies. His family may also be punished. Have students write about what their thoughts would be in trying to make the best of a horrible choice. Encourage them to try to be as honest as possible.

Creative Extensions—Held in Jail

Activity 7

In 1822, South Carolina passed the Negro Seaman's Act. It required all free African Americans on vessels docking in Charleston, South Carolina, to be jailed upon arrival until their vessel left the harbor. If, upon departure, the sailor or captain was unable or unwilling to pay the room and board expenses incurred during the incarceration, the freeman could be sold into slavery. These powerful legal obstructions, combined with rising prejudice, combined to exclude black seamen from merchant ships that stopped in southern ports.

On April 22, 1823, Amos Daley of Kingston, Rhode Island, arrived in Charleston, South Carolina, as an apprentice to Captain Rose of the schooner *Fox*. Under the new Negro Seaman's Act, Daley was jailed for thirteen days and then told never to return again. Daley was of mixed ethnicity, his mother being a Narragansett Native American. When the *Fox* returned six weeks later, the Charleston magistrates thought they had let him off easy when this free seaman and resident of the state of Rhode Island was given twelve lashes on his bare back.

Have students imagine they are African or African American and master harpoonists who have shipped out on whalers since they were sixteen years old. It is the year 1823. They just returned from a two-year whaling voyage on the *Black Warrior* out of New London, Connecticut. This trip has not been a financially successful one, and none of the crew is on very good terms with the captain. The boat has docked in Charleston, South Carolina, to offload and sell one hundred barrels of sperm oil. Suddenly, the harbormaster and a local sheriff come on board to remove them and several of their crewmates to a holding cell in the local jail. They've been held for a week, and they just found out that the *Black Warrior's* captain has refused to pay the charges for the cost of keeping them in jail. Citing financial losses, he has made arrangements through contacts of that same local sheriff to sell them to a plantation owner in Barbados, the West Indies. Have students work in groups to write the script for this event and then either perform it live or videotape it. Students will likely need to conduct further research to have the necessary information to complete the project.

Further Student and Teacher Resources

"Blacks in Whaling." *Footsteps*. Peterborough, NH: Cobblestone Publishing, May/June 1999.

Bolster, Jeffrey. *Black Jacks: African Americans in the Age of Sail*. Cambridge, MA: Harvard University Press, 1997. (an extremely thorough treatment for a teacher who wants to build a curriculum unit)

Music Connection

✣

Sea shanties accompanied work on board ship. "A good song was worth more than ten men on a rope," was a common saying. Ideas for sea shanties were borrowed from folk lyrics of seafaring people all over the world. Features strongly associated with traditional African music, such as repeating refrains as well as call and response, are a significant part of sea shanties. It is interesting to note that it was considered "taboo" to sing shanty style outside of the hard work of pushing, pulling, lifting, and hauling. When men were relaxing, different types of songs were sung, such as ballads.

> O, I'm going to leave her,
> Shallow-oh, Shallow Brown.
> O, I'm going to leave her,
> Oh, Shallow-oh, Shallow Brown.
> Ship on board a whaler.
> Shallow-oh, Shallow Brown.
> Ship on board a whaler.
> Oh, Shallow-oh, Shallow Brown.
> Ye are me only treasure,
> Shallow-oh, Shallow Brown.
> I love ye to full measure,
> Oh, Shallow-oh, Shallow Brown.

Compose your own sea shanty, which relates to the work of your daily life. Think about your hard work or your difficult struggles to do something. Try to use the traditional African features of "call and response" and "repeated refrains."

Diamond, Arthur. *Paul Cuffe: Merchant and Abolitionist*. New York: Chelsea House Publishers, 1989.

McKissack, Patricia, and Frederick McKissack. *Black Hands, White Sails: The Story of African-American Whalers*. New York: Scholastic, 1999.

Available Online

Hughill, Stan. *Shanties from the Seven Seas*. Mystic, CT: Mystic Seaport Museum, 1994, or "Sea Chanteys and Sailors' Songs" by Stuart M. Frank. KWM Monograph Series No. 11. (help to get started singing shanties in the classroom: **http://store.yahoo.com/kwm/seachanandsail.html**)

Malloy, Mary. *From Boston Harbor We Set Sail: A Curriculum Unit on African-American Mariners and Maritime Communities in Massachusetts*. (for Grades 5 and 6)

———. *African Americans in the Maritime Trades: A Guide to Resources in New England*. (both available at: **http://store.yahoo.com/kwm/fromcurunona.html**)

Websites

www.seacoastnh.com/blackhistory/jacks.html *Interview with Jeffrey Bolster, author of* Black Jacks: African American Seamen in the Age of Sail

http://cobblestonepub.com/pages/teideaslessonFOOTWhaling.html *Cobblestone's Footsteps' "Blacks In Whaling" issue, including Teachers' Guide to issue*

www.nha.org *Nantucket Historical Association*

www.whalingmuseum.org *New Bedford Whaling Museum, extensive information on the whaling industry*

www.whalingmuseum.org/kendall/heros/index_h.html *"Heroes in the Ships": African Americans in the Whaling Industry*

www.mysticseaport.org/welcome.html *Mystic Seaport*

www.mysticseaport.org/public/education/cuffe.html *Paul Cuffe Memorial Fellowship for the Study of Minorities in American Maritime History*

Contemporary Connection

※

Doors of Opportunity

For African Americans in the colonial period and in the early years of the Republic, going to sea offered opportunities. The whaling industry afforded black men the chance to travel, to become an integral part of a crew, and to earn a decent wage. However, going to sea also meant risking their lives, because no one could assure the outcome of a journey. African Americans continue to break barriers when they embark on some contemporary careers. Dr. Mae Jemison became the first African American woman to travel into outer space in 1992. To find out more about her life and her work with NASA, visit "Women of NASA" at *www.quest.arc.nasa.gov* or read her autobiography, *Find Where the Wind Goes: Moments from My Life.*

Primary Source Materials for Lesson 7

2.7.1

Portrait of Absalom Boston

Absalom Boston began his sailing career as an ordinary seaman in 1800. He rose quickly through the ranks and by 1822 sailed from Nantucket as the captain of his own ship, with an all-black crew.

Courtesy of Nantucket Historical Association

2.7.2

Inventory and appraisal of Absalom F. Boston's estate, 1855

An Inventory of the state of Absalom Jr. Boston late of Nantucket, in the county of Nantucket, deceased, viz:

House of Settlement on York Street	$375.00
Store and Land under it, with fixtures [etc.]	$125.00
A piece of land on South side of York St. with a house, barn and shed there on standing	$200.—
The John Banks house, on South side of York St.	$250.—
One Mowing Lot about 164 rods	$150.—
Furniture [etc.] in West Front room	$15.—
Articles in Bed room adjoining	$12.—
Furniture [etc.] in East front room	$12.—
Articles in closet adjoining	$5.—
10 Silver Spoons	$3.—
Furniture in dining room	$4.—
do. in kitchen	$5.—
do. in East front chamber	$18.—
do. in back chamber	$4.—
do. in West Chamber & closet	$20.—
do. in Chamber adjoining above	$15.—
Articles in garrett	$10.—
Do. in garrett chamber	$12.—
Two watches at $25. @ 5$	$30.—
Articles in back shop	$5.—
2 carts at 12$ @ 5$	$17.—
chaise & harness	$10.—
cart harness & barn utensils	$1.50
one hay cutter	$3.00
cash	$50.—
Nantucket June 23, 1855	**$1351.50**

Fees $3.00

G. W. Cobb
Samuel G. Mitchell } Appraisers
Wm. R. Coffin

Hannah C. Boston Admt. Nantucket, Is. June 23 1855. Subscribed and affirmed to by the above named Administratrix. Before me, Geo. Cobb, Register of Probate.

2.7.3

Selected stanzas of the 72-verse song "Ballad of the Industry," about the 1822 whaling voyage

> Come all you noble colored tars
>   That plough the raging main
> Come listen to my story boys
>   A thing that is quite strange
>
> It was on the 12th of May my boys
>   Eighteen hundred and twenty two
> A schooner from Nantucket boys
>   With all a colored crew
>
> A. F. Boston was commander
>   And him we will obey
> We took our anchor on our bow
>   Intend to go to sea . . .

The full text of Document 2.7.3 is available on the CD-ROM.

2.7.4

Painting of whaleman about to harpoon a whale, 1835

The boatsteerer was responsible for bringing the whaleboat as close as possible to the whale while avoiding being hit by the mammal's huge tail flukes. In the background another whaleboat is towing a killed whale to the "mother ship." Smoke from the ship suggests other crew members are boiling blubber to extract the oil.

Courtesy of New Bedford Whaling Museum

2.7.5

Image of the crew list of the whaling brig *Elizabeth*, 1841

Although only twenty-one years old, Pardon Cook had already served as captain on two voyages on the Elizabeth. *This trip lasted a little over a year, and the whale ship returned with 260 barrels of highly prized spermaceti oil and 120 barrels of oil from the blubber of the whale.*

Courtesy of the National Archives

LESSON 8

Leadership and Community in Philadelphia

In the late eighteenth century, despite the ringing language of freedom in America's founding documents, African Americans living as free people in the North or the South were not permitted the same liberties as their white neighbors. This discrimination by white society quite naturally fostered the growth of black community organizations. In the late 1700s and early 1800s, the city of Philadelphia was home to two prominent African American ministers who contributed greatly to African American community building. Their names were Absalom Jones and Richard Allen.

Jones and Allen had both been born into slavery. Richard Allen was able to buy his freedom in 1783, and Absalom Jones was freed in 1784. Both became Christians through the teachings of the Methodist Church, and they led other African Americans to the Methodist faith. Both also led in the struggle to ensure equality for themselves and fellow African Americans.

In this struggle, building community was key. In the spring of 1787, led by Jones and Allen, African Americans in Philadelphia formed the Free African Society (FAS). The group was committed to work for the abolition of slavery. In addition, the society was dedicated to mutual aid "to support one another in sickness, and for the benefit of their widows and fatherless children."

During the yellow fever epidemic of 1793, when 10 percent of Philadelphians were "carried away," members of the FAS nursed many ill people (both black and white), buried them when they died, and arranged for the care of their orphaned children. After the city recovered, Mathew Carey, who ran the largest publishing house in Philadelphia, printed the story of the yellow fever epidemic. In his pamphlet, Carey repeated rumors that members of the FAS were profiteering from the emergency. Carey's motives for these accusations are unclear. The mayor of Philadelphia acted quickly to commend the FAS for their community service. And Jones and Allen published a response, documenting the courageous actions of black people and including an accounting of all expenses and payments. This publication, "A Narrative of the Proceedings of the Black People during the Late Awful Calamity in Philadelphia in the Year 1793 and a Refutation of Some Censures, thrown upon them in some late Publications," has been reprinted in full and is available from the Independence Park Visitor Center in Philadelphia as well as online (see *www.independencevisitorcenter.com*).

Absalom Jones and Richard Allen were members of St. George's Methodist Episcopal Church, a predominately white congregation. In 1792, after a church renovation to which black members had contributed time and money, white members met and decided that black members could no longer sit near white members but, rather, should all be seated in the newly constructed balcony. On the first Sunday after the renovations were completed, religious worship was disrupted to remove African Americans from their regular pews to the gallery of the church. In some instances, people were interrupted while kneeling in prayer. At this egregious treatment, the African American members walked out. This event confirmed for black church members that it would be difficult if not impossible to find respect, freedom, and independence within white congregations. Black leaders renewed their efforts, already underway, to create a separate black church. These efforts were aided by Benjamin Rush, a white physician, who had engaged members of the Free African Society to care for the sick during the yellow fever epidemic. Dr. Rush had been a supporter of the free black community for some time.

In July 1794, the African Episcopal Church of Philadelphia opened its doors. Many black Philadelphians followed Absalom Jones, who, with permission from the Episcopal Bishop of Philadelphia, became a lay leader and formed the Episcopal congregation around him. Richard Allen remained in the Methodist faith and in the same year (1794) formed his own church, the Bethel African Methodist Episcopal Church. In 1807, the Bethel Church added an "African Supplement" to its articles of incorporation, giving the church more control over its building and affairs. In 1816, Allen and four other congregations of African American Methodists from nearby cities joined forces to form a new denomination, the African Methodist Episcopal (A.M.E.) Church. The A.M.E. Church became the first fully independent black denomination in America.

One additional example of Richard Allen's contributions to the black community is his work to create educational opportunities. In 1795, Allen opened a school; sixty children enrolled. In 1804, he founded the "Society of Free People of Colour for Promoting the Instruction and School Education of Children of African Descent." By 1811, there were eleven such schools in the city of Philadelphia.

In 1833, Richard Allen published his autobiography, *The Life, Experience and Gospel Labours of the Rt. Reverend Richard Allen*. An abridged portion of this narrative, describing the early part of his life, is included with this lesson. A longer segment may be found on the website for *Africans in America*.

Free black Philadelphians were active in using the political process to petition against slavery. In 1799, with Absalom Jones taking the lead, seventy-one "People of Colour, Freemen within the City and Suburbs of Philadelphia" submitted a petition to their congressional representatives focused on slavery, the slave trade, and the "kidnapping . . . of our brethren that are free." The petitioners used language from the Declaration of Independence and the Bill of Rights to argue that black slavery was incompatible with American liberty.

Organizing Idea

African Americans of the late eighteenth and early nineteenth centuries were looking for equality, freedom, and respect from their fellow Americans. Northern cities offered more options for African Americans, but segregation remained and African Episcopal churches began not just as places for worship but also as vehicles for creating community. Their precursor, the Free African Society, served as a blueprint for community service and cultural growth. The religious and cultural autonomy achieved by the successful founding of these organizations by Absalom Jones and Richard Allen symbolized the institution building that took place in Philadelphia despite white hostility.

Student Objectives

Students will:

- learn the story of an African American leader from post-Revolutionary America, Richard Allen
- learn about the formation of the Free African Society and the structures it created to support and enhance the lives of the African American community
- understand that the formation of the Free African Society and the A.M.E. Church helped to strengthen the African American community
- examine the charges leveled against the African American community during the yellow fever epidemic of 1793
- consider how individuals choose to become leaders

Key Questions

- Who was Richard Allen? How did he come to be a leader?
- What functions did the Free African Society (FAS) serve? How can we understand the controversy around the FAS after the yellow fever epidemic?
- How did the A.M.E Church come to be founded?
- What is the significance of the formation of an all-black denomination in the early nineteenth century?
- How does knowing this history contribute to our understanding of post-Revolutionary America?

Primary Source Materials

DOCUMENT 2.8.1: Excerpts from the autobiography of the Rev. Richard Allen, *The Life, Experience, and Gospel Labors of the Rt. Rev. Richard Allen,* 1833

DOCUMENT 2.8.2: Preamble of The Free African Society, 1787

DOCUMENT 2.8.3: Excerpts from "A Narrative of the Proceedings of the Black People during the Late Awful Calamity in Philadelphia, in the Year 1793: and A Refutation of some Censures Thrown Upon them in some late Publications," 1794

DOCUMENT 2.8.4: Photograph of stained-glass window at Mother Bethel A. M. E. Church, Philadelphia

Supplementary Materials

ITEM 2.8.A: Additional vocabulary lists for primary sources

Vocabulary

adherence	censorious	preamble	tenets
amendment	imprudence		

Student Activities

Activity 1 — **Reading the Rev. Richard Allen's Autobiography**

In his *Appeal To the Coloured Citizens of the World*, David Walker wrote of Allen, "When the Lord shall raise up coloured historians in succeeding generations to present the crimes of this nation to the then gazing world, the Holy Ghost will make them do justice to the name of Bishop Allen."

Using this acclaim, together with the information found in the introduction to this lesson, Allen's autobiography (2.8.1), and the photograph of the commemorative window at the Mother Bethel Church (2.8.4), introduce students to Richard Allen. The excerpt from Richard Allen's autobiography provides information about his early life and his initial experiences with Methodism. Throughout the narrative the reader sees Allen evolve from a convert to a preacher and finally to a leader. Students can be encouraged to consider the factors that prompt Allen to assume a role of leadership in this newly formed church community. More information can be found on the PBS website *Africans in America*.

Read aloud the introductory section of the autobiography. Students can then read the remainder of the autobiography in small groups and create time lines that highlight Allen's life and growth from parishioner to preacher to leader of a new movement among African Americans.

Activity 2 — **Essay Writing—The Growth of a Leader**

Ask students to find evidence in the autobiography (2.8.1) that describes (1) how Allen supported himself, (2) situations when his race seemed to be an important factor, (3) situations when his race seemed to be less significant, and (4) his awakening concern for other African American members of his church. Write an essay answering these questions: What does Richard Allen's life story tell us about the growth of a leader? Can you find similar examples in today's world?

Discussion—Responding to Emergencies

Activity 3

To begin a class discussion, ask: Who helps your family during emergencies? Today, when there is an emergency, such as a natural disaster, an epidemic, or blizzard, there are a host of agencies that individuals and communities can turn to in order to receive assistance. During the eighteenth century, families, neighbors, and religious organizations provided assistance for those in need.

Ask students to generate (brainstorm) a list of agencies and organizations that provide support for individuals and communities during emergencies, i.e., natural disasters such as blizzards, floods, and hurricanes. What organizations provide assistance during large fires? What organizations provide information, support and care during medical emergencies (SARS, West Nile Virus epidemics, HIV-AIDS action, spreading of anthrax)? Ask students to compare present-day response to emergencies in the developed world with the level of response that can be offered when only families, neighbors, or religious organizations are available to provide assistance.

A Diagram—The Free African Society

Activity 4

In previous centuries there was often a disparity between the care and support given to whites and African Americans. Read aloud the "Preamble of the Free African Society" (2.8.2), and ask students to read the Articles in order to create a diagram that illustrates the organizational structure of the society. On the diagram include information that answers the following questions:

- ❖ Who is eligible to join?
- ❖ What are the responsibilities of members?
- ❖ What care will be given to the membership? Who will receive support and care?
- ❖ What restrictions are members expected to abide by?
- ❖ Why did the name include the word "free"?

Reading—In Defense of Members of the Free African Society

Activity 5

The "Narrative of the Proceedings of the Black People during . . . the Year 1793" (2.8.3) gives us information about the work done by the Free African Society during the yellow fever epidemic. We find, as well, some indication of the prejudice faced by the group. Ask students to read the narrative and make a list of the accusations against members of the Free African Society. What arguments do Jones and Allen use to counter the criticism of white community members? Which of the personal stories of those who gave assistance was the most effective? Explain why. (To understand the value of the money involved, students can check *http://eh.net/ehresources*.)

Activity 6   **A Speech—Words That Echo True Today?**

"God and a soldier all men do adore
In time of war, and not before;
When the war is over, and all things righted,
God is forgotten, and the soldier slighted"

What does this quotation mean? Why do Jones and Allen use it to end their narrative? Have there been other times in American history that these words may have been true? Ask students to write a speech to deliver in class linking this quote to another period in U.S. history with which they are familiar.

Activity 7   **Essay Writing—Leadership and Racism (may be used as an assessment exercise)**

Based on the three readings, discuss the issues of leadership, community support, and racism in eighteenth-century American society. Using examples from these three readings, have students write an essay expressing what they have learned about leadership in the African American community or racism in American society. Here are some questions to consider: What did Richard Allen and Absalom Jones observe and experience that made them take roles of leadership in the African American community? Who are African American leaders today? What are their concerns? How have they worked to strengthen the African American communities in which they live?

Music Connection

One of Richard Allen's first acts as A.M.E. minister was to publish a hymnal. "He consciously set about to collect hymns that would have a special appeal to the members of his congregation, hymns that undoubtedly were long-time favorites of black Americans," writes Eileen Southern in *The Music of Black Americans: A History* (p. 75). The hymnal does not include melodies, but among them is the hymn that begins "Behold the awful trumpet sounds." His congregation, continuing the African tradition of improvisation in music, soon added choruses and refrains of "their own composing." Southern believes that "My Lord, what a morning," was written in response to the hymn. No one knows when the term "spiritual" began to be used to describe religious folksongs of African Americans, but "My Lord, what a morning," is among the most loved.

After listening to the spiritual (available on the CD-ROM), students should consider religious text from their own traditions and try to paraphrase the words and then create a hymn or spiritual to express the meaning.

Further Student and Teacher Resources

Anderson, Laurie Halse. *Fever 1793*. New York: Simon and Schuster Books for Young Readers, 2000.

Franklin, John Hope, and Alfred A. Moss. *From Slavery to Freedom: A History of African Americans,* 8th ed. New York: Knopf, 2000.

George, Carol V. R. *Segregated Sabboths, Richard Allen and the Emergence of Independent Black Churches, 1760–1840*. New York: Oxford University Press, 1973.

Hildebrand, Reginald F. *The Times Were Strange and Stirring: Methodist Preachers and the Crisis of Emancipation*. Chapel Hill: Duke University Press, 1995.

Klots, Steve. *Richard Allen: Founder of the African Methodist Episcopal Church (Black Americans of Achievement)*. New York: Chelsea House, 1991.

Laichas, Tom, and Tom Ingersoll. *"This Will Never Be Submitted to . . . Without a Civil War," Congress Debates Slavery, 1790–1800* (a unit of study for grades 10–12). Los Angeles: UCLA, National Center for History in the Schools, 1991.

Nash, Gary. *Forging Freedom: The Formation of Philadelphia's Black Community 1720–1840.* Cambridge, MA: Harvard University Press, 1988, 1991.

Raboteau, Albert J. *Canaan Land: A Religious History of African Americans.* New York: Oxford University Press, 2001.

Wilmore, Gayraud S. *Black Religion and Black Radicalism: An Interpretation of the Religious History of African-Americans,* 3rd ed. Maryknoll, NY: Orbis Books, 1998.

Websites

www.pbs.org/wgbh/aia/part3/3h465.html

www.geocities.com/bobarnebeck/allen.html

www.amecnet.org

http://earlyamerica.com/review/spring97/allen.html *for an essay on Richard Allen by James Henretta*

Contemporary Connection

✣

Social Concerns of the A.M.E. Church Today

Even today, the African Methodist Episcopal (A.M.E.) Church is more than a religious organization; it creates community for African Americans across the country. Part of its current community activism involves promoting home ownership among parishioners. Clergy see homeowners as investing in their futures as well as creating and strengthening more self-sufficient communities.

Many African Americans have faced discrimination and unfair loan practices when trying to buy a house. White homeownership in 2000 was about 74 percent, whereas African American homeownership was about 48 percent, according to the U.S. Department of Housing and Urban Development ("Lenders Put Faith in Clergy to Push for Homeownership," *Boston Sunday Globe*, April 13, 2003).

The A.M.E. Church has partnered with government mortgage companies such as Fannie Mae, which have agreed to provide loans to low- and middle-income families in major cities around the country. The church spreads the word of these opportunities to the people it serves and helps them find the resources they need.

In Pittsburgh, under the leadership of the Rev. Samuel Ware, the A.M.E. is trying to restore trust by ensuring that the black community will not be victims of excessive fees or higher interest rates, and it strives to provide greater fiscal and community investment for the members of the church. The A.M.E. Church continues to work actively for the betterment of its community. In cities from Philadelphia and Washington, D.C., to Los Angeles, it continues its original mission of community service and cultural growth.

Students can discover and share with the class the ways in which religious congregations in their communities become involved with social issues. How are needs identified? How are problems addressed?

Primary Source Materials for Lesson 8

2.8.1

Excerpts from the autobiography of the Rev. Richard Allen,
*The Life, Experience, and Gospel Labors of the
Rt. Rev. Richard Allen*, 1833

A number of us usually attended St. George's church in Fourth street; and when the colored people began to get numerous in attending the church, they moved us from the seats we usually sat on, and placed us around the wall, and on Sabbath morning we went to church and the sexton stood at the door, and told us to go in the gallery. He told us to go, and we would see where to sit. We expected to take the seats over the ones we formerly occupied below, not knowing any better.

Meeting had begun, and they were nearly done singing, and just as we got to the seats, the elder said, "Let us pray." We had not been long upon our knees before I heard considerable scuffling and low talking. I raised my head up and saw one of the trustees, H-M-, having hold of the Rev. Absalom Jones, pulling him up off of his knees, and saying, "You must get up—you must not kneel here." Mr. Jones replied, "Wait until prayer is over." Mr. H- M- said "No, you must get up now, or I will call for aid and force you away." Mr. Jones said, "Wait until prayer is over, and I will get up and trouble you no more." With that he beckoned to one of the other trustees, Mr. L-S to come to his assistance. He came, and went to William White to pull him up. By this time prayer was over, and we all went out of the church in a body, and they were no more plagued with us in the church.

The full text of Document 2.8.1 is available on the CD-ROM.

2.8.2

Preamble of The Free African Society, 1787

Philadelphia [12th, 4th mo., 1787]—Whereas, Absalom Jones and Richard Allen, two men of the African race, who, for their religious life and conversation have obtained a

119

good report among men, these persons, from a love to the people of their complexion whom they beheld with sorrow, because of their irreligious and uncivilized state, often communed together upon this painful and important subject in order to form some kind of religious society, but there being too few to be found under the like concern, and those who were, differed in their religious sentiments; with these circumstances they labored for some time, till it was proposed, after a serious communication of sentiments, that a society should be formed, without regard to religious tenets, provided, the persons lived an orderly and sober life, in order to support one another in sickness, and for the benefit of their widows and fatherless children."

Articles

"[17th, 5th mo., 1787]—We, the free Africans and their descendants, of the City of Philadelphia, in the State of Pennsylvania, or elsewhere, do unanimously agree, for the benefit of each other, to advance one shilling in silver Pennsylvania currency a month; and after one year's subscription from the date hereof, then to hand forth to the needy of this Society, if any should require, the sum of three shillings and nine pence per week of the said money: provided, this necessity is not brought on them by their own imprudence . . . .

The full text of Document 2.8.2 is available on the CD-ROM.

2.8.3

Excerpts from "A Narrative of the Proceedings of the Black People during the Late Awful Calamity in Philadelphia, in the Year 1793: and A Refutation of some Censures Thrown Upon them in some late Publications," 1794

Early in September, a solicitation appeared in the public papers, to the people of colour to come forward and assist the distressed, perishing, and neglected sick; with a kind of assurance, that people of our colour were not liable to take the infection. *[People at that time thought that people of African descent couldn't catch yellow fever. That proved to be untrue.]* Upon which we and a few others met and consulted how to act on so truly alarming and melancholy occasion. After some conversation, we found a freedom to go forth, confiding in Him who can preserve in the midst of a burning fiery furnace, sensible that it was our duty to do all the good we could to our suffering fellow mortals. We set out to see where we could be useful. The first we visited was a man in Emsley's alley, who was dying, and his wife lay dead at the time in the house, there were none to assist but two poor helpless children. We administered what relief we could, and applied to the overseers of the poor to have the woman buried. We visited upwards of twenty families that day—they were scenes of woe indeed! The Lord was plentiful to strengthen us, and removed all fear from us . . .

The full text of Document 2.8.3 is available on the CD-ROM.

2.8.4

Photograph of stained-glass window at Mother Bethel A. M. E. Church, Philadelphia

This stained-glass window honors the memory of the founder of the Mother Bethel Church in Philadelphia.

LESSON 9

Thomas Jefferson and His Responders

Thomas Jefferson: Icon and Contradiction

The inability of Thomas Jefferson to reconcile his private interests in slavery with his philosophical belief in liberty remains an enduring enigma for students of U.S. history. Recent information reveals those contradictions in Jefferson to be not only intellectual, but behavioral as well. It suggests that the author of the Declaration of Independence was a man who asserted publicly that "The slave, who is made free, might mix with, without staining the blood of, his master," and fathered children by his bonded slave-mistress. Yet he did not free his slave children, even upon his death. This adds another layer of complexity to the American statesman and scholar.

Aside from his work on the founding documents, Thomas Jefferson wrote and published only one book. His *Notes on the State of Virginia* is today seen as the best source of information about Jefferson's interests and views. First published in 1787, the book offers views on topics ranging from geography to government, science and education. It is in this book that Jefferson expresses his ideas and conflicts on race and specifically on the abilities (or lack thereof) of "negros."

The book was widely read at the time, and Jefferson's racial views caused widespread criticism, particularly among abolitionists. A selection of their writings is included with this lesson. Benjamin Banneker, a black Marylander with strong interests and skill in mathematics and science, wrote to Jefferson to prove him wrong. An early nineteenth-century figure, David Walker, the black author of passionate essays against slavery, urged his fellow blacks to stand up to Jefferson and not rely on white abolitionists to stand up for them.

The Story of Benjamin Banneker

Benjamin Banneker's grandmother, Englishwoman Molly Welsh, worked as an indentured servant in Maryland for seven years. At the end of her indenture, she purchased and farmed land. In time, she purchased two slaves, one of whom, Bannaka, she freed and later married. Benjamin's mother was born free because her mother was white. She married an enslaved African from Guinea who worked on a neighboring plantation. Born in 1732, Benjamin was taught to read and write by his grandmother. Later he attended an interracial school run by the Quakers, who would be from then on his constant friends, although he never joined the Society.

Benjamin Banneker grew up as a tobacco farmer and retained that occupation throughout his life. He never married. He was devoted to things mechanical and mathematical and pursued these self-taught avocations as a lifelong learner. Later, he developed an interest in astronomy, and with the help of a like-minded Quaker neighbor, Andrew Ellicott, he read and studied widely in this field, frequently borrowing books from Ellicott. With this knowledge and accurate mathematical computations of the positions of the sun, moon, and stars, in 1791 he produced the first of several almanacs. He correctly forecast solar and lunar eclipses, the precise rising and setting of the sun and moon, and tide tables for the region. Banneker's work so impressed Ellicott that he recommended Banneker to replace him as "scientific assistant" on the presidential commission to plan the construction of the nation's capital. Acting on the recommendation, Secretary of State Thomas Jefferson secured from President George Washington the appointment of Banneker to this post in the winter of 1791.

Benjamin Banneker died in October of 1806 at age seventy-four and was buried in the Ellicott family cemetery. He bequeathed all his papers and books to his friend, Andrew Ellicott.

David Walker's Appeal

David Walker was born in North Carolina in 1785, the son of an enslaved father and a mother who was free. The law in North Carolina at the time stated that children would inherit the status of their mother; thus David Walker lived his life as a free person.

As a young man, he traveled widely in the South, seeing the mistreatment of slaves and resolving to fight against the institution. He traveled also to other parts of the United States, meeting many of the social reformers of his day. At the age of forty-one, Walker settled in Boston, where he ran a clothing store and spent many hours reading, studying, and writing. He both distributed and wrote for *Freedom's Journal*, the abolitionist paper published by Samuel Cornish and John Russwurm. In 1829, he completed and circulated his own project, *The Appeal to the Coloured Citizens of the World*.

The Appeal was widely read and discussed among white as well as black people. Southern slaveholders were frightened for many reasons, not the least of which was that Walker advocated armed struggle to end slavery. James Turner in his introduction to the Appeal notes that "From 1829 until his death in 1830, David Walker was the most controversial and most admired Black person in America." Walker's work never went out of circulation and provided a foundation for black nationalism as well as Pan-Africanism.

Organizing Idea

In *Notes on the State of Virginia*, Thomas Jefferson described his doubts about the mental abilities of "negros." Advanced by so prominent a citizen, the question stimulated widespread debate. This lesson examines what Jefferson said and how other Americans, black and white, responded to his views.

Student Objectives

Students will:

- consider attitudes about race in eighteenth-century United States
- see how Benjamin Banneker used his prominence to defend all black people against racial stereotypes
- consider whether Banneker's action was a significant or a symbolic act by examining Thomas Jefferson's reply
- consider how David Walker's response differs from that of Benjamin Banneker

Key Questions

- What contradictions exist in Thomas Jefferson's writing, including the Declaration of Independence?
- What major arguments did others—black and white—present on the issue of race?

Primary Source Materials

DOCUMENT 2.9.1: Excerpts from *Notes on the State of Virginia* by Thomas Jefferson, 1787

DOCUMENT 2.9.2: Excerpts from the writings of white antislavery supporters

DOCUMENT 2.9.3: Benjamin Banneker's letter to Thomas Jefferson, August 17, 1791

DOCUMENT 2.9.4: Thomas Jefferson's reply to Benjamin Banneker, August 30, 1791

DOCUMENT 2.9.5: Excerpts from Article I. "Our Wretchedness in Consequence of Slavery," in *David Walker's Appeal To the Coloured Citizens of the World*, 1830

Supplementary Materials

ITEM 2.9.A: Additional vocabulary lists for primary sources

ITEM 2.9.B: A Historical Head

Vocabulary

almanac	endow	inalienable	oppression
brethren	faculty		

Student Activities

Read and Discuss—Thomas Jefferson's Writing

Activity 1

Individually or as a class, read the Declaration of Independence. Make a list of the major statements about freedom, liberty, and equality. Now read the excerpt from *Notes on the State of Virginia* (2.9.1).

- In what ways do Jefferson's questions and statements in his *Notes* conflict with the words and ideas in the Declaration of Independence?
- How could he be the author of both?
- Do you think he was speaking only for himself in *Notes*?
- Do we have any evidence that he was conflicted about what he was saying about "negros"?

Read and Discuss—Other White Views

Activity 2

As a class, students read the arguments put forward by other white men (2.9.2) who objected to the way Thomas Jefferson described the abilities of black people and identify the major points these men made. What factors might have made it possible for them to see what Jefferson seems not to have seen?

Read and Discuss—An Exchange of Letters

Activity 3

Have students work in small groups or in pairs to read the letter from Benjamin Banneker to Thomas Jefferson (2.9.3) and, also, Jefferson's reply (2.9.4).

- What was Banneker saying to Jefferson?
- How did he use Jefferson's own words to make his point about liberty and equality?
- How did he describe the institution of slavery? What do you think was Banneker's intent in writing to Jefferson?

Writing a Letter

Activity 4

Students should write a letter either to Jefferson, in response to the excerpt from *Notes on the State of Virginia,* or, taking the voice of Thomas Jefferson, to Benjamin Banneker, in response to his letter.

Activity 5   **David Walker's Views—Biographical Head**

Students read the excerpts from David Walker (2.9.5) in small groups; then using the outline of a head (Item 2.9.B), students create a picture showing the feelings and opinions of David Walker about slavery and Thomas Jefferson's views. On the back of the picture, students write their ideas in sentences. Allow time for the sharing of work.

Activity 6   **Research Extension—The Men Behind the Words**

Using books and the Internet, students research the lives of Thomas Jefferson, Benjamin Banneker, and David Walker and write brief, descriptive biographies for each of the men. Alternatively, students can create detailed posters that capture the key aspects of each man's life. These projects should be shared aloud, posted in the room, or assembled into a book to have as a classroom resource. (Sourcebook 3 includes a full lesson on David Walker.)

Activity 7   **Time Line**

Through research for the biographies, students should identify dates for significant events in the lives of these men and create a classroom time line, which they should continue to develop as new information is discovered. The time line can include major events in American history.

Activity 8   **Comparison—Racial Stereotyping**

Students compare the racial stereotyping that occurred in the eighteenth and nineteenth centuries with examples that can be found in the media today. How is it similar and how has it changed?

Activity 9   **Homework Math Challenge**

Ask students to explore the Friends of Benjamin Banneker organization (online at *www.thefriendsofbanneker.org*). The Friends of Benjamin Banneker Historical Park and Museum, Inc., is a nonprofit community organization founded to provide well-researched educational, historical, and cultural programs and exhibits regarding the life of Banneker. Challenge students to solve the puzzles found on the site. They will need to know the relationship between shillings and pounds and be prepared to deal with the nonstandard spelling common in that time period.

Further Student and Teacher Resources

Bendini, Silvio A. *The Life of Benjamin Banneker: The First African-American Man of Science.* Baltimore: Maryland Historial Society, 1999.

Jefferson, Thomas. *Notes on the State of Virginia.* Published for the Institute of Early

American History and Culture at Williamsburg, Virginia by the University of North Carolina Press, 1955. (edition used; there are others available)

Jordan, Winthrop D. *White Over Black, American Attitudes Towards the Negro, 1550–1812.* Chapel Hill: The University of North Carolina Press, 1968.

Kaplan, Sydney and Emma Nogrady Kaplan. *The Black Presence in the Era of the American Revolution 1770–1800.* Amherst: The University of Massachusetts Press, 1973.

Percoco, James. *A Passion for the Past.* Portsmouth, NH: Heinemann Publishers, 1998.

Walker, David. *David Walker's Appeal, In Four Articles; Together With A Preamble, To the Coloured Citizens of the World, but In Particular, and Very Expressly, to Those of the United States of America, Third and Last Edition, Revised and Published By David Walker, 1830.* Reprinted with an introduction by James Turner. Baltimore, MD: Black Classic Press, 1993.

Websites

www.thefriendsofbanneker.org *a time line of Banneker's life and the mathematical puzzles*

www.math.buffalo.edu/mad/special/banneker-benjamin.html *additional information on mathematicians of the African diaspora*

http://gwpapers.virginia.edu/articles/slavery *information on George Washington and slavery*

www.loc.gov/exhibits/treasures/trr022.html *site for American Treasures of the Library of Congress*

www.common-place.org *See July 2001 issue.*

www.besthistorysites.net/ *Click on U.S. history, then on Constitution. There are two sites on Jefferson.*

www.pbs.org/Jefferson/archives/interviews/frame.htm

Contemporary Connection

Understanding Historical Perspective

Thomas Jefferson remains an enigmatic figure today. He is revered as a founding father, a literate and elegant writer, the author of what we want to believe about liberty and equality. Yet he kept slaves throughout his life because he couldn't imagine life without them, and in recent years, the suspicion that he may have fathered children by one of his slaves, Sally Hemings, has surfaced again. In 1998, *Nature* magazine published a story of the DNA testing of Jefferson descendents that seemed to indicate that, in fact, he could have been the father of Sally Hemings' last child. That study generated the formation of groups to defend Jefferson's reputation and writings by historians attempting to sort out fact from myth. A balanced presentation of this issue can be found at *www.monticello.org//plantation/hemings-jefferson_contro.html*.

But the issues with which students of history wrestle are bigger than questions concerning Sally Hemings. In her book, *Thomas Jefferson and Sally Hemings: An American Controversy*, Annette Gordon-Reed describes a mock trial staged in 1994 by the New York Bar. Charles Ogletree served as prosecutor, Drew Days was the defense attorney; William Rehnquist was the judge. Gordon-Reed states, "The issue to be decided by the trial was whether examples of hypocrisy in Jefferson's life significantly diminished his contributions to American society." For an interesting essay on this debate, see *www.common-place.org* and search for *"Of Racism and Remembrance."*

It is helpful to remember that how we respond to Jefferson doesn't depend alone on his life and writings. The legacy of Thomas Jefferson for each of us is filtered through our own experiences, views, and beliefs. Students might discuss what makes a hero. Can someone be a hero, even a role model, while at the same time be inconsistent in his or her beliefs and actions?

Primary Source Materials for Lesson 9

2.9.1

Excerpts from *Notes on the State of Virginia* by Thomas Jefferson, 1787

In general, their existence appears to participate more of sensation than reflection.... Comparing them by their faculties of memory, reason and imagination, it appears to me, that in memory they are equal to the whites; in reason much inferior, as I think one could scarcely be found capable of tracing and comprehending the investigations of Euclid; and that in imagination they are dull, tasteless, and anomalous.... It will be right to make great allowances for the difference of condition, of education, of conversation, of the sphere in which they move.... Most of them indeed have been confined to tillage, to their own homes and their own society; yet many have been so situated that they might have availed themselves of the conversations of their masters.

The full text of Document 2.9.1 is available on the CD-ROM.

2.9.2

Excerpts from the writings of white antislavery supporters

William Pinkney, speaking before the House of Delegates in Maryland in 1789, said that Negroes and whites were "endued with equal faculties of mind and body . . . in all respects our equals by nature; and he who thinks otherwise has never reflected, that talents, however great, may perish unnoticed and unknown, unless auspicious circumstances conspire to draw them forth, and animate their exertions in the round of knowledge . . . . Thus the ignorance and the vices of these wretches are solely the result of situation, and therefore no evidence of their inferiority.

The full text of Document 2.9.2 is available on the CD-ROM.

2.9.3

Benjamin Banneker's letter to Thomas Jefferson, August 17, 1791

This, [the Revolutionary period] Sir, was a time when you clearly saw into the injustice of a state of slavery, and in which you had just apprehensions of the horrors of its condition. It was now that your abhorrence thereof was so excited, that you publicly held forth this true and invaluable doctrine, which is worthy to be recorded and remembered in all succeeding ages: "We hold these truths to be self-evident, that all men are created equal; that they are endowed by their Creator with certain unalienable rights, and that among these are, life, liberty, and the pursuit of happiness." Here was a time, in which your tender feelings for yourselves had engaged you thus to declare, you were then impressed with proper ideas of the great violation of liberty, and the free possession of those blessings, to which you were entitled by nature; but, Sir, how pitiable is it to reflect, that although you were so fully convinced of the benevolence of the Father of Mankind, and of his equal and impartial distribution of these rights and privileges, which he hath conferred upon them, that you should at the same time counteract his mercies, in detaining by fraud and violence so numerous a part of my brethren, under groaning captivity and cruel oppression, that you should at the same time be found guilty of that most criminal act, which you professedly detested in others, with respect to yourselves.

The full text of Document 2.9.3 is available on the CD-ROM.

2.9.4

Thomas Jefferson's reply to Benjamin Banneker, August 30, 1791

Sir,

I thank you sincerely for your letter of the 19th. instant and for the Almanac it contained. No body wishes more than I do to see such proofs as you exhibit, that nature has given to our black brethren, talents equal to those of the other colours of men, & that the appearance of a want of them is owing merely to the degraded condition of their existence both in Africa & America. I can add with truth that no body wishes more ardently to see a good system commenced for raising the condition both of their body & mind to what it ought to be, as fast as the imbecillity of their present existence, and other circumstance which cannot be neglected, will admit. I have taken the liberty of sending your almanac to Monsieur de Condorcet, Secretary of the Academy of Sciences at Paris, and member of the Philanthropic society because

I considered it as a document to which your whole colour had a right for their justification against the doubts which have been entertained of them. I am with great esteem, Sir, Your most obedt. humble servt.

Th. Jefferson

2.9.5

Excerpts from Article I. "Our Wretchedness in Consequence of Slavery," in *David Walker's Appeal To the Coloured Citizens of the World*, 1830

Oh! pity us we pray thee, Lord Jesus, Master.—Has Mr. Jefferson declared to the world, that we are inferior to the whites, both in the endowments of our bodies and of minds? It is indeed surprising, that a man of such great learning, combined with such excellent natural parts, should speak so of a set of men in chains. I do not know what to compare it to, unless, like putting one wild deer in an iron cage, where it will be secured, and hold another by the side of the same, then let it go, and expect the one in the cage to run as fast as the one at liberty . . . .

They think because they hold us in their infernal chains of slavery, that we wish to be white, or of their color—but they are dreadfully deceived—we wish to be just as it pleased our Creator to have made us . . . How would they like for us to make slaves of, and hold them in cruel slavery, and murder them as they do us?—But is Mr. Jefferson's assertions true? viz. "that it is unfortunate for us that our Creator has been pleased to make us *black*." We will not take his say so, for the fact. The world will have an opportunity to see whether it is unfortunate for us, that our Creator *has made us* darker than the *whites* . . . .

The full text of Document 2.9.5 is available on the CD-ROM.

LESSON 10

Resistance and Revolts by the Enslaved

White Americans have often asked why there were no slave rebellions in the United States similar to those that occurred in Haiti and other European colonies in the Americas. African Americans know that this is not quite the right question: there *were* slave rebellions in the United States. Slavery was no more tolerable here than elsewhere, and enslaved people took whatever opportunities were offered to resist, escape, and revolt. However, in the United States slaves were less successful in organizing large-scale uprisings and at maintaining the freedom they had seized than were slaves in other nations. The main reason why slave rebellions in the United States did not succeed—and often were prevented—was the extraordinary degree of police power exerted to control slaves' movements, contacts with one another, and communication with free people of color. This police power was deployed by local, county, and state governments, which were dominated by large planters but included poor white men; it backed up the power wielded directly by slaveowners with "patrollers" to chase runaways, with jailings and beatings for those who stubbornly resisted and trials and public hangings for those who dared to organize rebellions. This policy was triggered by the largest slave revolt in the Americas, the revolution in Haiti, and by the slave rebellions that the Haitian Revolution inspired in the United States.

What made the Haitian Revolution so revolutionary was that, first, enslaved African and Afro-Caribbean people liberated themselves and destroyed the institution of slavery and, second, that the leader Toussaint L'Ouverture, of African descent, succeeded in uniting black slaves, people of color, and whites to defend their national independence against European colonial powers. On January 1, 1804, Dessalines, one of Toussaint L'Ouverture's generals, proclaimed the independence of "Hayti," the native people's word for a mountainous place. Haiti was not only the second European colony in the Americas to declare its independence, but the first free black nation in this hemisphere.

People in the United States watched developments in Haiti closely. Slaveholders and many white political leaders in both North and South opposed Toussaint and feared that slave revolts would be contagious: African Americans inspired by the example of Haiti might rise up against their masters. Although such fears were often exaggerated, they were not unfounded, and whites took steps to avert slave revolts. Because Haitian refugees entered the United States through Charleston and New Orleans, southern states passed laws prohibiting immigration from St. Domingue in 1793. Slaveholders were horrified by Haiti's successful war for and declaration of independence. Fear was not confined to the South or to slave states: in 1805, whites drove black people away from the Fourth of July celebration at Philadelphia's Independence Hall.

African Americans did find inspiration in the example of Haiti, although they had their own reasons for rebellion. Uprisings led by Gabriel Prosser in Richmond, Virginia, in 1800; by Charles Deslondes in the vicinity of New Orleans, Louisiana, in 1811; and by Denmark Vesey in Charleston, South Carolina, in 1822, were all directly modeled on the Haitian Revolution. After these uprisings were put down militarily, slave owners and white political leaders shifted from considering plans for gradual emancipation to erecting legal systems to control and repress both free and enslaved African Americans. Direct contacts between Haitians and African Americans, as well as the inspiring example of Haitian independence, continued to be influential through the early nineteenth century and beyond. Black seamen who visited West Indian ports brought back news about the revolution, and some Haitians migrated to American seaports; in places such as Boston, New York, and Philadelphia, people and news from Haiti played keys roles in abolitionist activities. The anniversaries of Caribbean emancipation and Haitian independence were celebrated both before and after the Civil War. In the twentieth century, Toussaint L'Ouverture was remembered as a black hero, serving, for example, as the subject of a stunning series of paintings by the great African American artist Jacob Lawrence.

Gabriel Prosser

Gabriel and Martin Prosser were slaves to a tavern owner named Thomas Prosser in Virginia. The brothers were powerful speakers and avid readers; Martin was a preacher and Gabriel, an intellectual. Together, they read aloud to groups of slaves, sharing the news of the successful slave revolution that had taken place on Haiti. Gabriel adopted Toussaint's philosophy of racial and social equality, seeking allies among working-class white people. At funerals and weddings, they recited Bible stories about how God had delivered the children of Israel from slavery in Egypt. If slaves could be delivered to freedom in Haiti and in Egypt, they could come out of Virginia as well. Deliberately and methodically, Gabriel and Martin were sowing the seeds of rebellion among the enslaved around Richmond. They consigned their brother Solomon to make weapons for the planned rebellion. Approximately one thousand enslaved African Americans were recruited for their plan to take and hold Richmond.

The date for the uprising was set for August 30, 1800. Rain began to pour down at noon that day, flooding streets, creeks, and rivers and washing out bridges. Although Gabriel tried to call off the action, he could not get word out to everyone involved. Two slaves, Pharoah and Tom, may have told their master about the plot before it could be initiated. He informed Governor James Monroe, who called out the militia and quickly rounded up the suspected participants. Authorities captured Gabriel, who had escaped on a ship, the *Mary,* and returned him to Richmond. He refused to reveal anything about the revolt, and on October 7, 1800, the state hanged him along with fifteen other rebels. Twenty-one were reported to have been executed prior to this, and four more were scheduled to die after October 7. A precise number of those executed cannot be given with certainty, but at least thirty-five African Americans were hanged, four condemned blacks escaped from prison, and one committed suicide in prison. Other black participants were sold out of state.

Charles Deslondes

New Orleans was a racially diverse city, comprising numerous native peoples, such as the Catawba and Natchez, Africans and people of African descent, and white people of various European nationalities, mostly French, because the area was once a French colony. The city had strong ties with and similarities to Saint Domingue. Like Haiti, the New Orleans and southern Louisiana area also maintained sugar cane, indigo, and rice-growing plantations. Whites in power in Louisiana were very concerned about the possibility of rebellion spreading from Haiti.

Charles Deslondes was a free black man of Haitian descent. In 1811, he organized a group of five hundred enslaved people, with the intent of capturing New Orleans. Arming themselves with farm tools, they marched on the city, burning fields and plantations along the way. This constituted the largest slave uprising in American history. Confronted by the militia outside New Orleans, they fought for eleven days before they were defeated and captured.

Seventy-five slaves were held for questioning; investigations took one week. Twenty-five slaves were tried by a tribunal comprised of five plantation owners, some of whom had suffered property damage during the uprising. Eighteen of the condemned slaves were taken to their owners' plantations, shot, and beheaded, their heads impaled on poles along the road from New Orleans for sixty miles, as an example to remaining slaves.

Denmark Vesey

Records are not clear about whether Denmark Vesey was born in Africa or on a Caribbean island. A slave trader owned him, and for fourteen years Vesey traveled with the trader to many countries, living in Haiti for a time. He could read, write, and speak several languages. In 1800, the year of Gabriel Prosser's unsuccessful revolt, Vesey purchased his freedom with money he won in a lottery. As a free black man, he settled in Charleston, South Carolina, and became a successful carpenter. Vesey, like Gabriel Prosser, was inspired by the Haitian Revolution.

A devout member of the African Methodist Episcopal Church, Vesey committed himself to the establishment of a black church not controlled by whites. Within a few years, about six thousand black people had joined A.M.E. churches in Charleston. Fearful of large congregations of blacks gathering anywhere for any reason, white leaders planted spies in the congregations to report back their activities. In 1821, Charleston authorities shut down the A.M.E. church for no announced reason. This act launched Denmark Vesey's rebellion: "We were deprived of our rights and privileges by the white people . . . our church was shut up so that we could not use it . . . it was high time for us to seek our rights . . . and we were fully able to conquer the whites if we were only unanimous and courageous as the Santo Domingo [Haitian] people were."

At the center of the conspiracy were free blacks and people of color, sailors, and skilled tradesmen. An estimated nine thousand men were involved. To prevent the full disclosure of the scheme should one of the leaders confess or be caught, each of Vesey's lieutenants was only entrusted with part of the plan. Vesey alone knew the complete plan. However, it began to fall apart when a house slave revealed what was afoot to his master. Some of the leaders confessed and named others. When the full extent of the plot was discovered, horrified community leaders requested federal troops to help bring the slaves under control. Vesey and the leaders of his revolt were arrested and tried. Like Gabriel Prosser, Vesey refused to discuss the plot or to implicate others. On July 3, 1822, South Carolina authorities hanged Denmark Vesey. Of the 131 slaves arrested, 35 were executed and 37 were exiled from the United States. Because city officials suspected that some members of the Charleston Neck A.M.E. Church had played a role in the attempted insurrection, they burned the church to the ground.

Organizing Idea

The Haitian Revolution was the first successful slave rebellion and independence movement in the Americas led by people of African descent. It inspired African Americans to rebel and struck fear into white people. Slave owners and local governments took extraordinary measures to control the enslaved population. Yet African Americans went beyond individual acts of resistance to organize rebellions.

Student Objectives

Students will:

- ❖ understand how human abuse and tyranny provide the reason and rationale for revolutions great and small, successful and unsuccessful
- ❖ begin to understand the impulses of courage, commitment, and sacrifice for a cause
- ❖ explore the relationship between uprisings planned by the enslaved and the Haitian Revolution

Key Questions

- Has an enslaved individual the right to resist his owner?
- What might move an enslaved person to rebel?
- What would prompt a free man to lead a slave rebellion? What might he gain? Lose?
- What is a "terrorist"? Would any of the people in this lesson be described as terrorists? Who? Why or why not?
- Were slave revolts acts of "freedom fighters" pursuing wars of liberation, or were they simply crimes against society?
- Was revolution the proper way to resolve the conflict between the colonists and Great Britain in 1776? Was it the proper way to resolve the conflict between the enslaved and slaveholders? Why or why not?

Primary Source Materials

DOCUMENT 2.10.1: Solomon Prosser's confession, Virginia, September 1800

DOCUMENT 2.10.2: Thomas Jefferson's letter to James Monroe, September 20, 1800

DOCUMENT 2.10.3: Excerpt from *Travels in some parts of North American in the years 1804, 1805, & 1806*, by Robert Sutcliff

DOCUMENT 2.10.4: Image of a woodcut of an iron mask, collar, leg shackles, and spurs, 1807

DOCUMENT 2.10.5: Louisiana "Act providing for the payment of slaves killed and executed on account of the late insurrection in this Territory and for other purposes," April 25, 1811

DOCUMENT 2.10.6: Confession of Monday Gell, 1822

DOCUMENT 2.10.7: Excerpt from "Reflections, Occasioned by the late Disturbances in Charleston," a pamphlet anonymously written, October 1822

DOCUMENT 2.10.8: Excerpt from "Negro Plot: An Account of the Late Intended Insurrection Among a Portion of the Blacks of this City of Charleston, South Carolina" by James Hamilton, 1822

Supplementary Materials

ITEM 2.10.A: Additional vocabulary lists for primary sources

ITEM 2.10.B: An essay: "The Haitian Revolution"

Vocabulary

conspiracy	insurrection	rebellion	uprising

Student Activities

Background Essay—The Haitian Revolution

Activity 1

The Haitian Revolution was a long and complex affair, and its impact on African Americans was significant. Teachers may wish to supplement the introduction to this lesson with an essay describing the Haitian Revolution in more detail. (Item 2.10.B is available on the CD-ROM.) Students can read the essay themselves, or the teacher may wish to present a short lecture.

Discussion—A Confession

Activity 2

It was widely reported, including by James Monroe, who personally interviewed Gabriel Prosser, that Prosser never confessed. Monroe wrote of the conversation: "From what he [Prosser] said to me, he seemed to have made up his mind to die, and to have resolved to say but little on the subject of the conspiracy."

- What could have been Gabriel Prosser's reasons for not speaking?
- Students should consider parallels and differences regarding James Monroe's commitment to the American Revolution and Gabriel Prosser's commitment to abolish slavery.
- If Prosser never confessed, of what exactly was he guilty?
- How might the enslavement of Prosser and others have affected the outcome of the "trial" and the sentence imposed?

Students should read the confession of Gabriel Prosser's brother, Solomon (2.10.1).

- Why might Solomon have confessed?
- Would Solomon's confession and others' testimony have been reliable at the trial? Why or why not?
- What protections exist today that help prevent forced and/or false confessions?

Discussion—Thomas Jefferson's Response

Activity 3

Students should read the excerpt from Thomas Jefferson's letter (2.10.2). Ask students to create three columns on a piece of paper. In the left column, have them write down the alternatives that Jefferson noted for handling the imprisoned African Americans. In the middle column, have them write what Jefferson thinks about each choice. In the right column, the students should write their opinion regarding each alternative. Students should also add their own suggested alternatives. Discuss the results as a class. Then address the following questions:

- As a slaveowner himself, why was Thomas Jefferson concerned about "where to stay the hand of the executioner"?
- What does Jefferson mean by "the rights of the two parties?" Is he indicating that slaves had rights in this situation?

Activity 4 **Interviews with Key Characters**

After reading the excerpt from Robert Sutcliff's work (2.10.3), the class should discuss the following questions:

- From the excerpt, can you determine what Sutcliffe's attitude was toward slavery?
- How might his attitude affect what he wrote?
- What effects would the Prosser uprising have on Virginia in the years that followed?
- Why might the lawyer have shared with Sutcliff the quote from one of the condemned slaves?
- What is your reaction to the defendants' words? Was the Prosser uprising similar to Americans rebelling against Great Britain? Was this man's trial a "mockery"?

Now ask the students to assume roles. They can choose to be interviewers or individuals from that era—Gabriel Prosser, Solomon Prosser, the lawyer Sutcliff refers to, Robert Sutcliff, James Monroe, or Thomas Jefferson. To prepare for the interviews, students will need to conduct some additional research on the uprising and the specific individual they are interviewing or "becoming."

Activity 5 **Discussion—Restraints Used on the Enslaved**

Ask students to examine the images of restraints commonly used to punish enslaved African Americans. Students are likely to have strong emotional responses to these disturbing images. As a class, discuss why slaveowners would use things like this. The woodcut was created in 1807. Were the devices a result of the uprising or one of the contributing causes? Ask students to imagine working on a plantation while wearing something like this. What are the many different ways an enslaved person might have reacted to such a form of punishment? Why do you think Thomas Branagan wrote his poems and illustrated them with this woodcut? Do you think images like this can make a difference on how people think of slavery? Students can read parts of the poems on *www.time.com/time/sampler/article/0,8599,423941,00.html*.

Activity 6 **Reading and Analyzing—The Aftermath of the New Orleans Uprising**

The Deslondes uprising took place January 8, 1811, and was crushed days later. Students should read the act passed in the Louisiana Territory (2.10.5). Notice the date it was passed. What conditions led to this act being passed so quickly? What is the intent of the Act?

A number of enslaved African Americans connected with the uprising were tried. Students can check *www.lib.lsu.edu/special/purchase/history.html*, a website that lists many of the court cases. Students can then use the Internet to research these court cases to develop an understanding of these trials and sentences. How were they similar to and different from those in other slave uprisings?

Gell's Confession

Activity 7

Students should read Monday Gell's confession (2.10.6). Discuss as a class:

- Why did Gell confess, and why might he have offered such a complete confession?
- How might Monday's confession have been delivered: under torture? Do you think he spoke with pride, disdain, courage, or fear?
- What made Gell name others, condemning some while protecting others, claiming ignorance of the conspiracy? How many individuals did he implicate?
- How can students find out what happened to Gell?

Reading an Explanation for the Vesey Uprising

Activity 8

Students should read the excerpt from the pamphlet (2.10.7) and address these questions:

- Why might this pamphlet have been written anonymously?
- According to the author, what were the causes for the uprising?
- What might be a possible impact on the public of a publication such as this?
- Why are the injustices of slavery not mentioned?
- Which "causes" for the uprising do you think the author felt could be addressed?
- What is meant by "the powerful operation of the press"? Does that exist throughout history into modern times? What is the power of the press for both literate people as well as for those who cannot read?

Analyzing a Description of Denmark Vesey

Activity 9

After students read James Hamilton's description of Vesey (2.10.8), they should work in pairs or small groups.

- First, list the many words Hamilton uses to describe Denmark Vesey. How would you describe his choice of words? Are they neutral, derogative, or complimentary?
- What picture does Hamilton create of Vesey? How can you determine to what degree Hamilton's description of Vesey is accurate?
- Why do you think Hamilton might have written this?
- Why are there no records of Vesey's actual words?
- Vesey was a free man; how might that have affected his sentence?

Activity 10 **Writing Extension—Denmark Vesey's Statement**

Students put themselves in Denmark Vesey's place, following his arrest. They decide who the audience is and then write a statement. They can address the statement to the court, to the white population of Charleston, to free blacks, or to the enslaved.

Activity 11 **Research Extension—Maroon Communities**

For more than four centuries, thousands of enslaved Africans managed to escape from bondage into the wilderness, where they established freed societies that challenged the colonial establishment and often violently resisted slavery. They were a driving force in the fight against slavery and the dominant plantation economy in the Americas. The exhibition "Creativity and Resistance: Maroon Cultures in the Americas" at the Center for Folklife and Cultural Heritage at the Smithsonian Institution provides a look at this creative culture from the past all the way through the present. Through time lines, artwork, prints, documents, and music, teachers and students can experience the rich history and culture of the maroons. Go to *www.si.edu/maroon* for teacher's guides to the exhibit as well as other online resources.

Further Student and Teacher Resources

Basker, James. Poems excerpted from *Amazing Grace: An Anthology of Poems about Slavery, 1660–1810*. New Haven: Yale University Press, 2002.

Katz, William Loren. *Breaking the Chains: Afro-American Slave Resistance*. New York: Atheneum, 1990. Books II–III. (middle school)

McKissack, Patricia C., and Frederick L. McKissack. *Rebels Against Slavery*. New York: Scholastic, 1996. (middle school)

Music Connection

✠

Enslaved African Americans sang as they worked at a variety of monotonous tasks—picking cotton, stripping tobacco, or threshing rice. They sang to keep themselves alive in a brutal plantation economy. Their work songs might be solos, such as "Arwhoolie" (see Lesson 1), or ones that drew on the African traditions of call and response. Often the lead singer would improvise the lines; sometimes he or she would tell short action stories in their songs. "Long John" (available on the CD-ROM) continues the tradition of worksongs. Long John is escaping from slavery or perhaps from prison. Either way, he is long gone. Students should listen for the call and response style used and the added percussive sound. Consider how worksongs laid the foundation for both the blues and gospel music.

Websites

http://lsm.crt.state.la.us/cabildo/cabildo.htm *for background information on the Charles Deslondes case, "The Cabildo: Two Centuries of Louisiana History"*

http://etext.virginia.edu/journals/EH/EH36/poole1.html *to help students develop a greater understanding of the demographics of Charleston as a city of immigrants, Americans, enslaved and free black people, commerce and slave trading during the early 1800s, Vesey's time*

http://docsouth.unc.edu/church/hamilton/summary.html *for a full text of the official summary of Denmark Vesey's planned insurrection, "Negro Plot"*

For information on Haiti:

www.webster.edu/~corbetre/haiti/haiti.html

www.tfaoi.com/aa/1aa/1aa182.htm *traditional fine art online*

www.a-r-t.com/jacoblawrence/Louvertureweb/

Contemporary Connection

Who Were the Conspirators in the Vesey Case?

Early in the "Vesey Conspiracy" case, a number of Charleston, South Carolina, citizens questioned whether court proceedings violated basic justice, but their protests were ignored. For almost two hundred years, the case remained largely unexamined. In the October 2001 issue of *The William and Mary Quarterly*, historian Michael P. Johnson revisited the case. In his essay, he reviewed three recent books about the Vesey conspiracy. Johnson also read original manuscripts and court records and concluded that "the court for its own reasons, colluded with a handful of intimidated witnesses to collect testimony about an insurrection that, in fact, was not about to happen; that Denmark Vesey and the other men sentenced to hang or to be sold into exile were not guilty of organizing an insurrection." There was indeed a conspiracy, Johnson writes, "conjured into being in 1822 by the court, its cooperative black witnesses and its numerous white supporters and kept alive ever since by historians eager to accept the court's judgments while rejecting its morality."

In the January 2002 issue of the same publication, historian and book-review editor Robert A. Gross initiated a forum and invited other scholars, including the authors of books cited by Johnson in his article, to respond to this question: "Is it possible ever to determine the truth behind charges of slave plots when the evidence has been gathered by powerful whites who control the circumstances and set the terms by which the enslaved are allowed to speak, at the peril of their lives?"

Students can read both Johnson's article, "Denmark Vesey and His Co-Conspirators," and the Gross Forum, "The Making of a Slave Conspiracy, part 2," online at *www.historycooperative.org/journals*. Working in small groups, students can read the information, discuss the question raised by Gross, and then report the results of the discussions to the class as a whole.

Primary Source Materials for Lesson 10

2.10.1

Solomon Prosser's confession, Virginia, September 1800

Gabriel informed me, in case of success, that they intended to subdue the whole of the country where slavery was permitted, but no further.

The first places Gabriel intended to attack in Richmond were the Capitol, the Magazine, the Penitentiary, the Governor's house and his person. The inhabitants were to be massacred, save those who begged for quarter and agreed to serve as soldiers with them. The reason why the insurrection was to be made at this particular time was, the discharge of the number of soldiers one or two months ago, which induced Gabriel to believe the plan would be more easily executed.

Given under our hand this fifth day of September, 1800.

The full text of Document 2.10.1 is available on the CD-ROM.

2.10.2

Thomas Jefferson's letter to James Monroe, September 20, 1800

Where to stay the hand of the executioner is an important question. Those who have escaped from the immediate danger, must have feelings which would dispose them to extend the executions. Even here, where every thing has been perfectly tranquil, but where a familiarity with slavery, and a possibility of danger from that quarter prepare the general mind for some severities, there is a strong sentiment that there has been hanging enough. The other states & the world at large will forever condemn us if we indulge in a principle of revenge, or go one step beyond absolute necessity. They cannot lose sight of the rights of the two parties, & the object of the unsuccessful one. Our situation is indeed a difficult one: for I doubt whether these people can ever be permitted to go at large among us with safety. To reprieve them and keep them in prison till the meeting of the legislature will encourge [sic] efforts for their release. Is there no fort & garrison of the state or of the Union, where they would be confined, & where the presence of the garrison would preclude all ideas of attempting a rescue. Surely the legislature would pass a law for their exportation, the proper measure on this & all similar occasions? I hazard these thoughts for your own consideration only, as I should be unwilling to be quoted in the case; you will doubtless hear the sentiments of other persons & places, and will thence be enabled to form a better judgement on the whole than any of us singly & in a solitary situation.

2.10.3

Excerpt from *Travels in some parts of North American in the years 1804, 1805, & 1806,* by Robert Sutcliff

A lawyer who was present at their trials at Richmond, informed me that on one of them being asked, what he had to say to the court on his defence, he replied, in a manly tone of voice: "I have nothing more to offer than what General Washington would have had to offer, had he been taken by the British and put to trial by them. I have adventured my life in endeavouring to obtain the liberty of my countrymen, and am a willing sacrifice in their cause: and I beg, as a favour, that I may be immediately led to execution. I know that you have pre-determined to shed my blood, why then all this mockery of a trial?"

The full text of Document 2.10.3 is available on the CD-ROM.

2.10.4

Image of a woodcut of an iron mask, collar, leg shackles, and spurs, 1807

Thomas Branagan was a repentant Irish slavetrader who wrote two epic poems criticizing slavery. The autobiographical "The Penitential Tyrant; or, Slave Trader Reformed" was illustrated with a woodcut depicting a number of devices of punishment and torture. Branagan gave a copy of his epic poem to Thomas Jefferson.

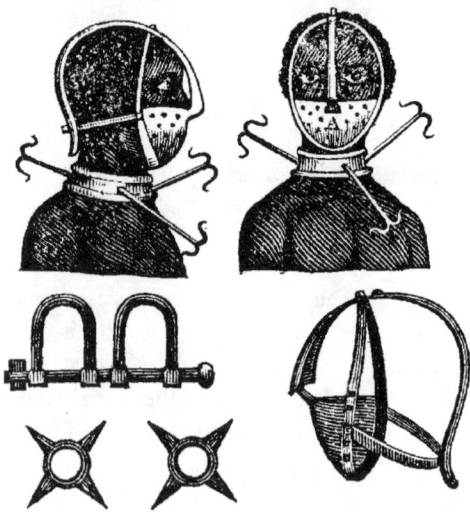

Courtesy of the Library of Congress

2.10.5

Louisiana "Act providing for the payment of slaves killed and executed on account of the late insurrection in this Territory and for other purposes," April 25, 1811

An Act providing for the payment of slaves killed & executed on account of the late insurrection in this territory and for other purposes.

Section 1:
Be it enacted by the [illegible] Council and House of Representatives of the Territory of Orleans in general assembly convened, that for each and every slave killed & executed on account of the late insurrection in this Territory, there shall be paid the sum of three hundred dollars.

Section 2:
And be it further enacted that one third of the appraised value agreeable to the appointment returned to the Governor, shall be paid for the dwelling Houses which were burnt by negroes during aforesaid insurrection,—and it shall be the duty of the Treasurer of the Territory to pay out of any monies in the Treasury and otherwise appropriated on the warrant of the Governor, the several sums which this act [illegible].

April 25th 1811

William C.C. Claiborne,
Governor of the Territory of Orleans

2.10.6

Confession of Monday Gell, 1822

Albert Inglis came to me and asked if I knew any thing about [the plan]; I said yes. He asked me if I had joined; I said yes; he said he was one also; he said Adam, a free man wanted to see me, I went with him one night; Adam asked me how many men had joined; I told him what Frank Ferguson had said; he asked me if I believed it; I said yes; he said if he could only find men behind him he would go before. Previous to the 16th, Albert said to me quit the business, I told him I was too far into it, so I must stick to it.

 I never wrote to St. Domingo or any where else on this subject, nor kept a list or books, nor saw any such things, but heard that Paul William had a list nor did I hear any thing about arms being in possession of the blacks. I don't know that Tom Russel make pikes, nor that Gullah Jack had any of them.

The full text of Document 2.10.6 is available on the CD-ROM.

2.10.7

Excerpt from "Reflections, Occasioned by the late Disturbances in Charleston," a pamphlet anonymously written, October 1822

Previous to the proposal of any plan for preventing the recurrence of similar danger, it may be useful to advert to the causes which produced the late conspiracy. The following may be assigned as some of the most obvious:—1st, The example of St. Domingo, and (probably) the encouragement received from thence.—2dly, The indiscreet zeal in favor of universal liberty, expressed by many of our fellow-citizens in the States north and east of Maryland; aided by the Black population of those States.—3dly, The idleness, dissipation, and improper indulgencies permitted among all classes of the Negroes in Charleston, and particularly among the domestics: and, as the most dangerous of those indulgencies, their being taught to read and write: the first bringing the powerful operation of the Press to act on their uninformed and easily deluded minds; and the latter furnishing them with an instrument to carry into execution the mischievous suggestions of the former.—4th, The facility of obtaining money afforded by the nature of their occupations to those employed as mechanics, draymen, fishermen, butchers, porters, hucksters, &c.—5th, The disparity of numbers between the white and black inhabitants of the City. No effort of ours can remove some of these causes, but over others we may exercise control.

2.10.8

Excerpt from "Negro Plot: An Account of the Late Intended Insurrection Among a Portion of the Blacks of this City of Charleston, South Carolina" by James Hamilton, 1822

In 1800, Denmark drew a prize of $1500 in the East-Bay-Street Lottery, with which he purchased his freedom from his master, at six hundred dollars, much less than his real value. From that period to day of his apprehension he has been working as a carpenter in this city, distinguished for great strength and activity. Among his colour he was always looked up to with awe and respect. His temper was impetuous and domineering in the extreme, qualifying him for the despotic rule, of which he was ambitious. All his passions were ungovernable and, savage; and to his numerous wives and children, he displayed the haughty and capricious cruelty of Eastern Bashaw. He had nearly effected his escape, after information had been lodged against him. For three days the town was searched for him without success. As early as Monday, the 17th, he had concealed himself. It was not until the night of the 22d of June, during a perfect tempest, that he was found secreted in the house of one of his wives. It is to the uncommon efforts and vigilance of Mr. Wesner, and Capt. Dove, of the City Guard, (the latter of whom seized him) that public justice received its necessary tribute, in the execution of this man. If the party had been one moment later, he would, in all probability, have effected his escape the next day in some outward bound vessel.

The full text of Document 2.10.8 is available on the CD-ROM.

Colonization: A Close Look at a Complex "Solution"

LESSON 11

The ideal of equality emerged as a central principle during the American Revolution. Yet Native Americans, imported Africans, and new immigrants such as the Irish were not treated with dignity and respect; all these groups were treated as despised races, and their "natural rights" were disregarded. Building meaningful national unity required closing the enormous gap between the philosophical ideal of equality and the brutal reality of slavery and racial discrimination that existed in the United States.

Many white Americans could not imagine a racially mixed society with free African Americans living and working alongside them and enjoying equal citizenship rights. Freedom and blackness were, to many whites, entirely incompatible; once slavery was defined in terms of race, free blacks were a contradiction in terms. Even whites who wished to abolish slavery sought a solution to the "problem" posed by free black people. The idea of deporting those African Americans who had been emancipated was proposed in the early eighteenth century. Its proponents suggested establishing colonies in the Caribbean or Africa where freed slaves could be resettled. During the Revolutionary War, the British established Sierra Leone, the center of their African slave trade, as a refuge for some black Loyalists who had supported the British side in exchange for the promise of freedom.

After the Revolution, prominent American leaders, most white but some black, advocated colonization. The American Colonization Society was organized in 1816. All its founders were white; the majority were slaveowners, others were not. Among the founders were James Madison, Francis Scott Key, Daniel Webster, and Henry Clay. Most of the money they raised came from private contributions. Later, Congress and the legislatures of Maryland and Virginia also contributed money. Colonization was intended not only to rid the United States of free black people, but also to bring the Christian religion to Africa and to generate trade between the two continents. In 1822, the Colonization Society established the nation of Liberia, which in 1846 became an independent republic.

Some African Americans embraced the concept of moving to Africa because they despaired of attaining equality in the United States. More than 12,000 African Americans emigrated to Liberia with the assistance of the American Colonization

Society. However, the idea of colonization met determined resistance from many prominent black leaders. Among the most outspoken was Richard Allen, a former slave who, after purchasing his freedom, became a Methodist preacher and founded the African Methodist Episcopal Church in Philadelphia. (See Lesson 8.) Allen's congregation at Bethel A.M.E. understood that the promotion of voluntary emigration of free black people was based as much on a desire to get rid of them as it was on benevolence. African Americans were two centuries removed from Africa, and most had no desire to move to what was, for them, a foreign land. Allen expressed the belief that free black people should stay in America to do what they could for their enslaved brothers and sisters. Moreover, he said, "this land, which we have watered with our tears and our blood, is now our mother country."

Organizing Idea

Colonization meant the resettlement of freed African Americans in Africa or other places outside the United States. The American Colonization Society and its goals were viewed by some as a panacea for the problem of race relations, but others viewed this plan as a denial of equal rights for black Americans.

Student Objectives

Students will:

- analyze colonization as a policy designed to solve the problem of free black people in a society marked by slavery and racial discrimination
- learn about the role that slavery and emancipation played in creating the countries of Liberia and Sierra Leone
- understand the major arguments for and against colonization

Key Questions

- What was the American Colonization Society trying to accomplish? Were their goals altruistic?
- Why were some African Americans interested in moving away from the United States?
- What evidence do we have of people's actual experiences after moving to one of the West African colonies?
- What were the principal arguments for and against colonization?

Primary Source Materials

DOCUMENT 2.11.1: Letter written by Capt. Paul Cuffe to Mr. Mills, 1816

DOCUMENT 2.11.2: Excerpts from the "First Annual Report of the Colonization Society," January 1818

DOCUMENT 2.11.3: Image of a membership certificate for the Colonization Society

DOCUMENT 2.11.4: Excerpts from a petition from the American Colonization Society, "A Memorial to the United States Congress," 1820

DOCUMENT 2.11.5: Excerpts from James Madison's "Plan for the Emancipation of the Slaves," June 15, 1819

DOCUMENT 2.11.6: Abraham Camp's letter to Elias B. Caldwell, July 13, 1818

DOCUMENT 2.11.7: Excerpt from a Circular Forwarded by a Committee of the Inhabitants of Monrovia, to Their Brethren in the United States

DOCUMENT 2.11.8: Map of the West Coast of Africa from Sierra Leone to Cape Palmas, including the colony of Liberia

DOCUMENT 2.11.9: Excerpts of a letter from Richard Allen, *Freedom's Journal*, Nov. 2, 1827 (Vol. 1, No. 34)

DOCUMENT 2.11.10: Richard Allen's "Address to the Free People of Colour of These United States," September 1830

DOCUMENT 2.11.11: Frederick Douglass, "Colonization," *The North Star*, January 26, 1849

DOCUMENT 2.11.12: Excerpts from *Reflections on the Causes that Led to the Formation of the Colonization Society*, 1832

DOCUMENT 2.11.13: Excerpts from August Washington's letter to the *New-York Daily Tribune:* "Liberia As It Is . . . III," June 27, 1854

Supplementary Materials

ITEM 2.11.A: Additional vocabulary lists for primary sources

ITEM 2.11.B: Outline map of West Africa

Vocabulary

| civilized | emancipation | oppressor |
| colonization | manumission | prejudice |

Student Activities

Engaging the Students—What Was the Situation?

Activity 1

Using information from the introduction to this lesson, begin the study of colonization by asking students to think about the lives of free black people during the nineteenth century. Why might some African Americans be interested in leaving the United States, and why would others want to remain here? Throughout the nineteenth century, what reasons might whites have to want *free* blacks out of the country? Consider economic as well as social rationales.

Note: The documents in this lesson, all of which favor or defend colonization, use phrases and expressions unfamiliar to twenty-first-century students. It may be helpful to review vocabulary before beginning the readings.

Activity 2 **Reading—Supporters of Colonization**

Divide the class into five groups. Each group receives copies of a document. Group 1 reads the letter written by Paul Cuffe (2.11.1). A second group reads excerpts from the "First Annual Report of the Colonization Society" (2.11.2) and examines the membership certificate (2.11.3); group 3 reads "A Memorial (a petition) to the United States Congress" (2.11.4). Group 4 reads excerpts from James Madison's plan (2.11.5). The fifth group reads the letter from Abraham Camp, a free man of color (2.11.6) and the circular from the inhabitants of Monrovia (2.11.7). Each of these documents presents the colonization movement in a positive light, but their perspectives and reasons differ.

Students in each group should read with these questions in mind:

- ❖ What do the writers have to say about colonization?
- ❖ How do we know they are in favor of developing a colony in Africa for free black men and women?
- ❖ What problems do they hope to solve?
- ❖ Is their presentation convincing? Why or why not?

After reading and discussing the selections, each group should decide how to present the document(s) to the rest of the class. After all groups have presented, ask students to consider what they have learned about *why* the idea of colonization was attractive to some people, both black and white.

Activity 3 **Map Activity**

On an outline map of West Africa (Item 2.11.B), using an atlas as a reference, students highlight Sierra Leone and Liberia in color and label the bordering countries. Using an overhead transparency of the African continent, project and draw the map onto large chart paper; then have students trace the countries of Sierra Leone and Liberia on the paper. Students working in groups can draw in and label the major rivers, shade in and label the mountains and ocean, and label and locate contemporary cities and settlements.

Students can then compare and contrast their map with the nineteenth-century map (2.11.8). Where were the early settlements and why? (Another good source for outline maps is *www.nationalgeographic.com/xpeditions/atlas*.) Looking at the maps, consider what would have been the geographical advantages and disadvantages of these countries.

Reading—A Spokesman for Opponents of Colonization

Activity 4

Students should read the two documents by the Rev. Richard Allen (2.11.9 and 2.11.10). These texts can also be read aloud in class, either by the teacher or by one of the students. The speech would be particularly effective when presented in this manner.

Have students discuss how Allen's point of view differs from that reflected in the earlier documents. Is he in favor of colonization or not? What are his reasons? Ask students to pick a persona (white or black, male or female) and write a letter to Bishop Allen responding to his ideas. The letter can be shared with the class or placed on a bulletin board to be read by individuals on their own time.

Reading—Ongoing Opposition

Activity 5

Ask students to recall what they know about Frederick Douglass (also see Sourcebook 3, Lesson 10) Then ask for a volunteer to read his article aloud (2.11.11). What is the tone of the article? How does it differ from the writing of Richard Allen? What sentiments do Allen and Douglass express in common? By the time Douglass printed this article in *The North Star*, the idea of colonization had been considered, off and on, for many years. How might that fact have added to Douglass' attitude?

Douglass uses visual images in his writing. Ask students to create an illustration to go with this article.

What Was It Like in Liberia?

Activity 6

Together or individually, students read the excerpts from *Reflections on the Causes that Led to the Formation of the Colonization Society* (2.11.12), published in 1832. As these observers describe it, what was Liberia like? Make a list of all the positive attributes described. Next, read the letter written by August Washington in June of 1854 (2.11.13). How does this document differ from the first one? Make a list of all the problems that Washington sees. Compare your two lists. What has gone wrong? Was the planning faulty? Were people not well informed? Did some of the problems result from things over which people had no control? How was this colonial "frontier" similar to and different from the experience of people settling the West in this country in the nineteenth century?

Debate—For or Against Colonization

Activity 7

As a culminating activity for this lesson, have students use what they have discovered to debate the pros and cons of colonization for African Americans. Set the debate in the 1830s (the arguments changed over time) and imagine a setting where both black and white people have gathered. Students may adopt the identities of actual people or imagine historical identities for themselves. It is important for students to consider their character's race, sex, geographical location, and perhaps their occupation and religious faith, because people's social position shaped their views on such controversial questions. You may want to consider allowing female students to play the roles of male speakers, white students the roles of black speakers, and vice versa. (At that time, women rarely spoke in public.)

After the debate, ask students to return to the twenty-first century and analyze the arguments presented on both sides What factors might predispose black people to consider emigration? What might predispose white people to support or oppose colonization? How has our society addressed the issues raised in the debates about colonization?

Further Student and Teacher Resources

"Liberia: Africa's First Republic." *Footsteps.* Vol. 3, No. 1 (January/February 2001).

Blaustein, Albert P., and Robert L. Zangrando, eds. *Civil Rights and the Black American: A Documentary History.* New York: Washington Square Press, a Division of Simon & Schuster, 1968.

Smith, James Wesley. *Sojourners in Search of Freedom: the Settlement of Liberia by Black Americans.* Lanham, MD: University Press of America, 1987.

West, Richard. *Back to Africa: a History of Sierra Leone and Liberia.* New York: Holt, Rinehart and Winston, 1971.

Wiencek, Henry. *The Hairstons: An American Family in Black and White.* New York: St. Martin's Press, 1999.

Wiley, Bell I. *Slaves No More: Letters from Liberia, 1833–1869.* Lexington, KY: University Press of Kentucky, 1980.

Websites

Emigrants to Liberia. Pontiac, MI: Christine's Genealogy Website.

http://ccharity.com/liberia/index.htm *Several links to primary documents about the establishment of the early colonies, including ships' passenger lists and constitutional documents.*

www.pbs.org/wgbh/aia/part3/3narr4.html

www.loc.gov/exhibits/african/afam002.html *Be sure to scroll through several of the next sections of the African-American Mosaic on the Library of Congress website, because the collection on colonization and Liberia is quite extensive.*

http://docsouth.unc.edu/church/liberian/menu.html

Contemporary Connection

※

Liberia Today

The PBS documentary *Liberia: America's Stepchild* follows the story of America's colonial legacy in that African nation. It begins with the colonization of Liberia by freed and former American slaves as a result of the efforts of the U.S. government and the American Colonization Society. The story continues by exploring the new colonists' relationship with the indigenous peoples. Finally, the program brings us up to date by examining the causes of civil strife that has plagued Liberia since 1980. Copies of the video may be ordered from *www.pbs.org*.

Students should be aware of current news stories about the long-term civil war in Liberia and peace efforts in that country. What is happening now? What is America's involvement? Ask students to weigh in on the debate about whether or not America has a responsibility to help the Liberians with nation building.

Primary Source Materials for Lesson 11

2.11.1

Letter written by Capt. Paul Cuffe to Mr. Mills, 1816

Agreeable to information given me by a citizen of Sierra Leone, the citizen has ever been desirous that a settlement should be established at that place, with those people that may come from America, he is a man of good character. The great River Congo, near the equator, its powerful population and goodness of soil, I hope will not always be neglected. I much approve of a vessel being sent as thou has mentioned.

In 1815, I carried out to S. Leone, nine families, 38 in number, and in 1816, I have had so many applications, that I believe I might have had the greater part to have carried out of Boston and the vicinity. I should think about Christmas, would be the most healthy season for a vessel to arrive on the coast. As to the length of the voyage, it would depend on the extent of discoveries to be made. I think from twelve to eighteen months, provided the voyage should extend to the Cape of Goodhope and the Tristan Islands . . .

The full text of Document 2.11.1 is available on the CD-ROM.

2.11.2

Excerpts from the "First Annual Report of the Colonization Society," January 1818

The Society have engaged two agents to explore the western coast of Africa, and to collect such information as may assist the Government of the United States in selecting a suitable district on that continent for the proposed settlement . . . .

The addition which has recently been made to our stock of knowledge of that continent . . . is highly encouraging to that enlarged and beneficent plan, which associates the political emancipation and future comfort of an unfortunate class of men, with the civilization and happiness of an afflicted, oppressed, and degraded quarter of our globe . . . .

An effort has been unfortunately made to prejudice the minds of the free people of color against this institution, which had its origin, it is believed, in an honest desire to promote their happiness . . .

2. The objection on the part of the coloured people, it is readily seen, springs from first impressions, and is the result entirely of ignorance and misapprehension. As these are removed, and their minds are informed upon the subject, the phantoms which their alarmed imaginations had conjured up gradually disappear; and when they learn that the land of their fathers is not cursed by a perpetual and unvarying sterility, nor inhabited by ferocious savages, that instinctive principle which binds it to their affections, is soon seen to unfold itself . . . The Managers are the more confirmed in this opinion from their knowledge of the (approval) of many of the most intelligent among the people of colour to the plan of the Society . . . , and that many of those, who were at first violent in their opposition, have become as decidedly friendly, upon learning the real motives, intentions and objects of the Society . . . .

The full text of Document 2.11.2 is available on the CD-ROM.

2.11.3

Image of a membership certificate for the Colonization Society

Selling life memberships was a standard method of fund-raising. The American Colonization Society charged $30. In 1825, one of the agents of the society who sold the certificates in New England estimated that approximately $50,000 had been raised in this way "into the treasury of the Lord." Notice the image in the seal that is the symbol for the society. It reads Lex In Tenebris *(law in darkness/shadows).*

Courtesy of the Library of Congress

2.11.4

Excerpts from a petition from the American Colonization Society, "A Memorial to the United States Congress," 1820

The last census shows the number of free people of color of the United States, and their rapid increase. Supposing them to increase in the same ratio, it will appear how large a proportion of our population will, in the course of even a few years, consist of persons of that description.

No argument is necessary to show that this is very far indeed from constituting an increase of our physical strength; nor can there be a population, in any country, neutral as to its effects upon society. The least observation shows that this description of persons are not, and cannot be, either useful or happy among us; and many considerations, which need not be mentioned, prove, beyond dispute, that it is best, for all the parties interested, that there should be a separation; that those who are now free may become so those who hereafter, should be provided with the means of attaining to a state of respectability and happiness, which, it is certain, they have never yet reached, and, therefore, can never be likely to reach, in this country . . . .

The full text of Document 2.11.4 is available on the CD-ROM.

2.11.5

Excerpts from James Madison's "Plan for the Emancipation of the Slaves," June 15, 1819

To be consistent with existing and probably unalterable prejudices in the United States, the freed blacks ought to be permanently removed beyond the region occupied by, or allotted to, a white population. The objections to a thorough incorporation of the two people are, with most of the whites, insuperable; and are admitted by all of them to be very powerful. If the blacks, strongly marked as they are by physical and lasting peculiarities, be retained amid the whites, under the degrading privation of equal rights, political or social, they must be always dissatisfied with their condition, as a change only from one to another species of oppression; always secretly confederated against the ruling and privileged class; and always uncontrolled by some of the most cogent motives to moral and respectable conduct. The character of the free blacks, even where their legal condition is least affected by their colour, seems to put these truths beyond question. It is material, also, that the removal of the blacks be to a distance precluding the jealousies and hostilities to be apprehended from a neighbouring people, stimulated by the contempt known to be entertained for their peculiar features; to say nothing of their vindictive recollections, or the predatory propensities which their state of society might foster. Nor is it fair, in estimating the danger of collision with the whites, to charge it wholly on the side of the blacks. There would be reciprocal antipathies doubling the danger . . . .

The full text of Document 2.11.5 is available on the CD-ROM.

2.11.6

Abraham Camp's letter to Elias B. Caldwell, July 13, 1818

I am a free man of colour, have a family and a large connection of free people of colour residing on the Wabash, who are all willing to leave America whenever the way shall be opened. We love this country and its liberties, if we could share an equal right in them; but our freedom is partial, and we have no hope that it ever will be otherwise here; therefore we had rather be gone, though we should suffer hunger and nakedness for years. Your honour may be assured that nothing shall be lacking on our part in complying with whatever provision shall be made by the United States, whether it be to go to Africa or some other place; we shall hold ourselves in readiness, praying that God (who made man free in the beginning, and who by his kind providence has broken the yoke from every white American) would inspire the heart of every true son of liberty with zeal and pity, to open the door of freedom for us also. I am, &c.

Abraham Camp.

2.11.7

Excerpt from a Circular Forwarded by a Committee of the Inhabitants of Monrovia, to Their Brethren in the United States

The first consideration which caused our voluntary removal to this country, and the object we regard with the deepest concern, was liberty—liberty in the sober, simple, but complete sense of the word—not a licentious liberty—nor a liberty without government, or which should place us without the restraint of salutary laws—but that liberty of speech, action and conscience, which distinguishes the free enfranchised citizens of a free state. We did not enjoy that freedom in our native country; and from causes, which, as regards ourselves, we shall soon forget forever, we were certain, it was not there attainable for our children or ourselves. We truly declare, that our expectations and hopes, in this respect, have been realized . . . .

LESSON 11: COLONIZATION: A CLOSE LOOK AT A COMPLEX "SOLUTION"

2.11.8

Map of the West Coast of Africa from Sierra Leone to Cape Palmas, including the colony of Liberia

The map was compiled chiefly from the surveys and observations of the Rev. Jehudi Ashmur and James Hamilton Young and was published in Philadelphia in 1830.

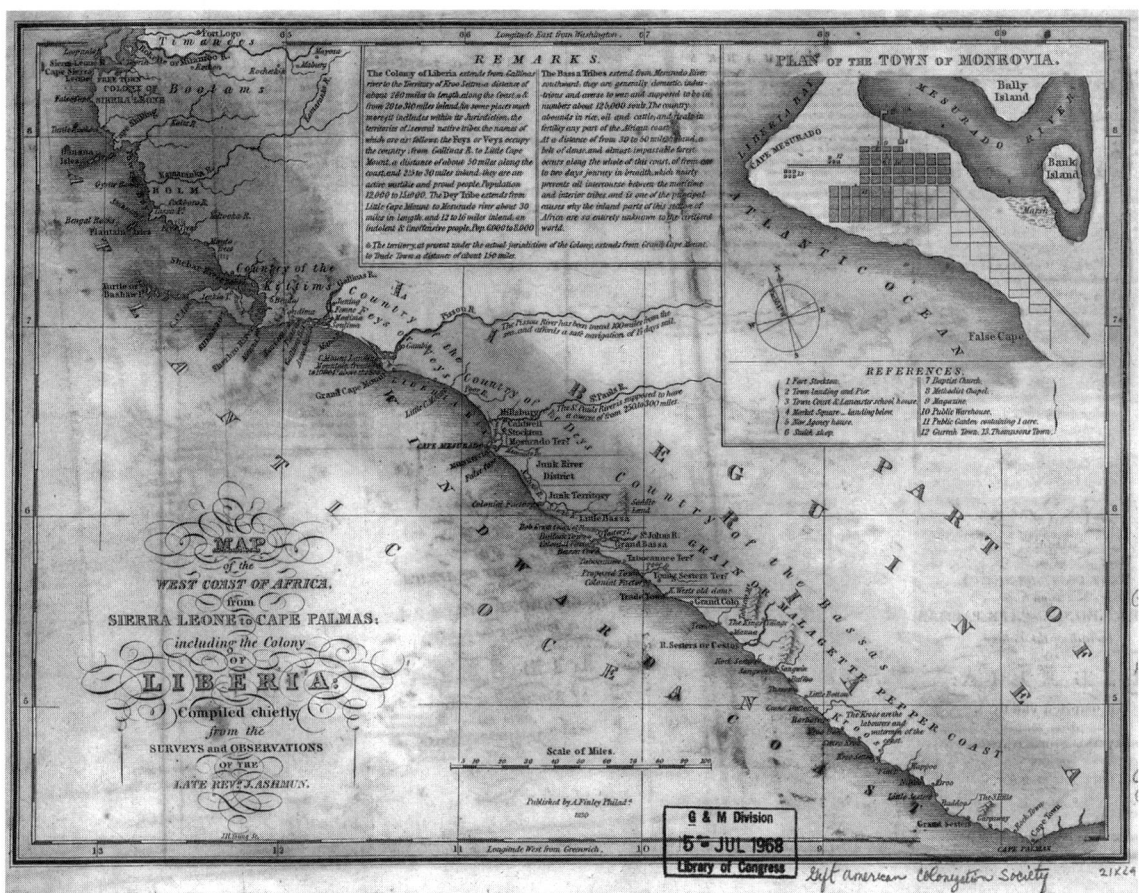

Courtesy of the Library of Congress

2.11.9

Excerpts of a letter from Richard Allen, *Freedom's Journal*, Nov. 2, 1827 (Vol. 1, No. 34)

Can we not discern the project of sending the free people of colour away from their country? Is it not in the interest of the slave-holders to select the free people of colour out of the different states, and send them to Liberia? Will it not make their slaves uneasy to see free men of colour enjoying liberty? It is against the law in some of the Southern States, that a person of colour should receive an education, under a severe penalty. Colonizationists speak of America being first colonized; but is there any comparison between the two? America was colonized by as *wise, judicious and educated* men as the world afforded. WILLIAM PENN was for *learning, wisdom, or intelligence*. IF all the people were as ignorant and in the same situation as our brethren, what would become of the world? Where would be the principle or piety that would govern the people? We were stolen from our mother country, and brought *here*. We have *tilled* the ground and made fortunes for thousands, and still they are not weary of our services. *But they who till the ground must be slaves*. Is there not land enough in America, or "corn enough in Egypt?" Why should they send us into a far country to die? See the thousands of foreigners imigrating to America every year: and if there be ground sufficient for them to cultivate, and bread for them to eat, why would they wish to send the *first tillers* of the land away? . . .

The full text of Document 2.11.9 is available on the CD-ROM.

2.11.10

Richard Allen's "Address to the Free People of Colour of These United States," September 1830

And in pursuit of this great object, various ways and means have been resorted to; among others, the African Colonization Society is the most prominent. Not doubting the sincerity of many friends who are engaged in that cause; yet we beg leave to say, that it does not meet with our approbation. However great the debt which these United States may owe to injured Africa, and however unjustly her sons have been made to bleed, and her daughters to drink of the cup of affliction, still we who have been born and nurtured on this soil, we, whose habits, manners, and customs are the same in common with other Americans, can never consent to take our lives in our hands, and be the bearers of the redress offered by that Society to that much afflicted country . . . .

[A] settlement in the British province of Upper Canada, would be a great advantage of the people of colour . . . .

The full text of Document 2.11.10 is available on the CD-ROM.

2.11.11

Frederick Douglass, "Colonization," *The North Star*, January 26, 1849

We are of the opinion that the free colored people generally mean to live in America, and not in Africa; and to appropriate a large sum for our removal, would merely be a waste of the public money. We do not mean to go to Liberia. Our minds are made up to live here if we can, or die here if we must; so every attempt to remove us will be, as it ought to be, labor lost. Here we are, and here we shall remain. While our brethren are in bondage on these shores, it is idle to think of inducing any considerable number of the free colored people to quit this for a foreign land.

For two hundred and twenty-eight years has the colored man toiled over the soil of America, under a burning sun and a driver's lash—plowing, planting, reaping, that white men might roll in ease, their hands unhardened by labor, and their brows unmoistened by the waters of genial toil; and now that the moral sense of mankind is beginning to revolt at this system of foul treachery and cruel wrong, and is demanding its overthrow, the mean and cowardly oppressor is meditating plans to expel the colored man entirely from the country. Shame upon the guilty wretches that dare propose, and all that countenance such a proposition. We live here—have lived here—have a right to live here, and mean to live here.—F.D.

2.11.12

Excerpts from *Reflections on the Causes that Led to the Formation of the Colonization Society*, 1832

The colonists in their address to the coloured population of the United States observe that the soil is not exceeded for fertility, or productiveness, when properly cultivated by any soil in the world. The hills and plains are covered with perpetual verdure. The productions of the soil go on through the year without intermission. Notwithstanding the imperfections of the farming tools used by the natives, they raise more than they can consume and frequently more than they can sell. "We have," they add, "no dreary winter here, for one-half the year, to consume the productions of the other half. Nature is constantly renovating herself and constantly pouring her treasures all the year round, into the lap of the industrious."

The full text of Document 2.11.12 is available on the CD-ROM.

2.11.13

Excerpts from August Washington's letter to the *New-York Daily Tribune:* "Liberia As It Is . . . III," June 27, 1854

When I published in THE TRIBUNE in 1851 my views in favor of African colonization, I could not believe that the opponents of the scheme had uttered so much truth. In that communication, the only thing I have since found to regret was my advocacy of the proposed line of steamers to this coast, and this regret is only for the reason that there is as yet no suitable preparation made for emigrants as to comfortable houses, and proper medical attendance, by the American Colonization Society nor the United States Government. Still I have charity enough to believe that if the former and latter knew these things as they are, if the Society was not able, the Government itself, for humanity's sake, would do something to aid them . . . . The state of things here, years ago, in regard to the treatment and suffering of emigrants was heart-rending and almost incredible, and yet no one who had not the means and opportunity to leave the country dared report them. They have greatly changed now for the better, and yet there is a dark chapter that never has been written. All the letters from Liberia, published in papers in the States give too high a coloring to everything pertaining to this country . . . .

The full text of Document 2.11.13 is available on the CD-ROM.

The Westward Expansion of Slavery and the Missouri Compromise of 1820

LESSON 12

The Missouri Compromise of 1820 postponed but did not resolve the conflict between slave and free states, which intensified as the United States expanded into the western territories acquired by the Louisiana Purchase of 1803. The contest for access to these lands was conducted between 1819 and 1821 in the halls of Congress, as representatives of southern slaveholders and of northern farmers sought to advance the competing interests of their constituents and to defend their differing definitions of liberty. The Missouri Compromise raised but did not settle questions of federal power to decide the future of slavery in the territories, the limits of settlers' power to exercise self-government, and the interpretation of Constitutional guarantees of liberty and property.

The Northwest Ordinance of 1787 established federal authority over new territories, defined the process for the creation of new states, and prohibited slavery in the territories acquired from Great Britain after the Revolutionary War. The ordinance was passed by Congress just before the drafting of the U.S. Constitution, and its principles were incorporated into that founding document. Although the ordinance allowed the recapture of fugitive slaves, it did not allow settlers in those territories to establish slavery. That provision was uncontroversial, because this northern region was regarded as unsuitable for plantation agriculture. But the Southwest Territory Act of 1790, which was modeled on the Northwest Ordinance, deliberately did not include any ban on slavery; that provision, too, was passed without any Congressional debate. This southern region, due west of existing slave states, was regarded as eminently suited to plantation agriculture. The practical effect of these two acts was to extend the Mason-Dixon line that divided Pennsylvania and Maryland westward to the Mississippi River. To the north, slavery was forbidden by an explicit federal policy; to the south, slavery was allowed implicitly.

The Louisiana Purchase included lands adjacent to both slave and free regions. President Thomas Jefferson had promised the French and Spanish who lived in the newly acquired territory "free enjoyment of their property." White residents believed that included the slaves they owned, although the federal government never explicitly agreed. Jefferson expressed the hope that slavery would eventually disappear, yet

163

he did nothing to ensure that slavery would not take root in the West. He did insist that the foreign importation of slaves be banned, but he knew that Congress would ban the international slave trade in 1808 in any case. When Congress organized the territories that became the states of Louisiana and Missouri, it followed the 1790 Southwest Territory Act. Northerners proposed a ban on slavery; they prevailed in the House but were defeated in the Senate. By 1812, when Louisiana was admitted to statehood, slavery was well established as far north as St. Louis. In 1819, when Missouri asked permission to write a state constitution, there were 10,000 slaves there—one-sixth of the territory's population.

The "Missouri crisis" was precipitated by Northerners' awareness that, if they did nothing to prevent Missouri from becoming a slave state, slavery would expand further north and the balance of power in Congress would shift toward the South. Mississippi (1817) and Alabama (1819) had been admitted as slave states, and Arkansas had been organized as a slave territory (1819). Northerners had only a slim majority in the House, and North and South held an equal number of seats in the Senate. The admission of Illinois as a nominally free state (1818) did not increase Northerners' power, because slavery was tolerated and even enforced there.

The Missouri Compromise divided the nation into two sections, one slave and one free. By enabling both North and South to expand their own systems into the West, it allowed Congress to avoid the issue for two decades. However, it sowed the seeds for future confrontation because the balance of power in the nation would shift with the addition of each new territory or state. Arguing the issue on Constitutional grounds also deepened the conflict: Southerners contended that the Constitution's protection of property was absolute and applied to property in slaves, whereas Northerners feared a southern conspiracy to take over the federal government. For two decades, northern congressmen gave up arguing that the Constitution's guarantees of freedom and republican government were meant to extend the blessings of liberty across the land; many seemed to accept the idea that the promises of the Declaration of Independence applied to white men only. But African Americans and their white abolitionist allies would not let the issue rest.

In 1820, few observers were as pessimistic about the long-term consequences of the Missouri Compromise as the elderly Thomas Jefferson. Writing from his retirement at Monticello, Jefferson declared that the Missouri Compromise would inevitably lead to disunion. "A geographical line, coinciding with a marked principle, moral and political, once conceived and held up to the angry passions of men, will never be obliterated." The dispute over Missouri, "like a fire-bell in the night, awakened and filled me with terror. I considered it at once the [death] knell of the Union." Jefferson's words were prophetic.

This lesson has two components. The first includes several documents that pertain to the Missouri Compromise of 1820. The second consists of letters that illuminate the experiences and perspectives of enslaved African Americans who were separated from their family and friends when their master took them west to Missouri.

Organizing Ideas

When the white residents of Missouri applied for admission to the Union as a slave state, Congress was divided over the future of slavery in the West. The Missouri Compromise of 1820 kept the issue off the national political agenda for two decades, but it also laid the basis for a bitter sectional division between slave and free states.

The expansion of slavery into the western territories affected enslaved African Americans profoundly, because families were separated as masters moved west or sold surplus slaves to traders who took them to newly developing regions. Slaves tried to keep in touch with their relatives and friends, and whenever possible they resisted being separated.

Student Objectives

Students will:

- learn how territorial expansion prolonged and institutionalized slavery in the United States
- understand the Congressional debate over the admission of Missouri into the Union as a slave state
- trace the significance of the Mason-Dixon line and the line of 36 degrees 30 minutes north latitude as geographical and political boundaries
- appreciate how the westward expansion of slavery affected slaves who moved with their masters or were sold to traders and sent to new territories
- discover how slaves felt about the family members and friends from whom they had been separated and how they resisted separation

Key Questions

- How did Missouri's application to enter the Union as a slave state divide the nation?
- Why were proposals to abolish or limit slavery in Missouri defeated?
- How did the Missouri Compromise preserve the balance of power between North and South?
- How did slaves respond to being taken to Missouri as their masters moved west?

Primary Source Materials

DOCUMENT 2.12.1: Excerpts from the Northwest Ordinance, July 13, 1787

DOCUMENT 2.12.2: The Tallmadge Amendment to Missouri's application for statehood, February 13, 1819

DOCUMENT 2.12.3: The Thomas Amendment to Missouri's application for statehood, February 17, 1820

DOCUMENT 2.12.4: Excerpts from the Missouri Enabling Act, March 6, 1820

DOCUMENT 2.12.5: Excerpts from the Constitution of Missouri, July 19, 1820

DOCUMENT 2.12.6: Resolution for the Admission of Missouri, March 2, 1821

DOCUMENT 2.12.7: Phil Anthony's letter to St. George Tucker, September 14, 1807

DOCUMENT 2.12.8: Cyfax Brown's letter to St. George Tucker, May 15, 1822

DOCUMENT 2.12.9: Phillis' letter to Mr. and Mrs. St. George Tucker, 1824

DOCUMENT 2.12.10: James Hope's letter to Mr. Beverly Tucker, November 16, 1834

DOCUMENT 2.12.11: Susan (Sukey) and Ersey's letter to Mr. Beverly Tucker, October 24, 1842

Supplementary Materials

ITEM 2.12.A: Additional vocabulary lists for primary sources

Student Activities

Activity 1 — Mapping the Results of Legislative Decisions

Using an outline map of the United States, students will

- draw in the thirteen original states and trace the Mason-Dixon line, which separated Pennsylvania, Maryland, and Virginia
- add the boundaries created by the Northwest Ordinance of 1787 (2.12.1)
- add the region acquired by the Louisiana Purchase in 1803
- draw the boundaries of the new state of Missouri and the line of 36 degrees, 30 minutes north latitude, observing how Missouri extended slavery to the north of where it had been banned by the Northwest Ordinance
- extend the line of 36 degrees, 30 minutes north latitude to the Pacific Ocean, seeing how it might have divided the West into slave and free territories.

Activity 2 — A Debate—A Slave State or Not?

Divide the class into a bicameral legislature, making sure that northern and southern senators are equally balanced but northern representatives have a slim majority in the House. Using Documents 2.12.2–2.12.6, reenact the debate over the admission of Missouri to the Union as a slave state. Individual students should play roles as Representatives James Tallmadge (New York), Timothy Fuller (Massachusetts), John W. Taylor (New York), and Jesse B. Thomas (Illinois), and—if their state existed in 1819–1820—whoever represented it in Congress. Other students need not play the roles of specific individuals but should represent specific states. Using the process of how a bill becomes a law, take these proposals from the House to the Senate and then negotiate the final compromise. Note that after Congress passes the Enabling Act, representatives of Missouri may participate in this reenactment.

Analyzing the Experiences of Slaves Held by the Tucker Family

Activity 3

Students should work in pairs or small groups to read (out loud) and analyze the letters from slaves held by the Tuckers (2.12.7–2.12.11). The questions will help them understand these slaves' experiences of moving to Missouri and their modes of addressing their "master." Give students time to respond to these letters emotionally; once they comprehend the language, they will be struck by the poignancy of the situations recounted. Equally important here is that students understand the language of deference, the way in which slaves might address their master in order to stress the obligations that the master owes to them and their expectations that a "good master" would do what they ask. In the last letter, in particular, the enslaved women seem aware that their request might be interpreted as defiance and attempt to cover it with flattery. Students should address the following questions.

Document 2.12.7: Phil Anthony's letter

- What were Phil's responsibilities on the plantation while his master was in the city?
- Consider the order in which he takes up different subjects. Why does he speak first about the health of the slaves? What other matters does he account for?
- Who sends messages via Phil Anthony's letter?
- Can you always distinguish between free or white people and slaves?
- Analyze the tone that Phil adopts in addressing St. George. Why does he close by calling himself "my dear master's dutiful servant"?

Note that, in early nineteenth-century America in general and Virginia especially, white people used the language of "master" and "servant" rather than "owner" and "slave."

Document 2.12.8: Cyfax Brown's letter

- Cyfax Brown begins by reminding St. George Tucker who he is. What was the Battle of Guilford, and what does Brown mean by saying that "I was then a man and a Servant to you"?
- What seems to have happened to Brown between 1781 and 1822? Recall that many slaves were emancipated by their masters after serving in the Revolutionary War.
- Why has Brown become impoverished? What does he ask from his former master?
- What does the last sentence suggest about possible contacts between Brown's family and Tucker?
- Why does he still call himself "your most humble Servant" in closing this letter?

Look back at Document 2.12.6, which required owners manumitting their slaves to "give security that the slave so emancipated will not become a public charge."

- Why were legislators concerned that elderly ex-slaves might become poor and depend on public welfare?
- Why did free black people have fewer rights than white people?

Document 2.12.9: Phillis' letter

- Why do you suppose Phillis addressed her letter to both Master and Mistress?
- How does she characterize them and their actions toward her?
- What is she asking them to do?
- Why does she prefer going to Missouri to remaining in Virginia?
- Why would she worry that her owners would think that her request meant that she is not "satisfied with" her "Situation of Life"?
- How does she attempt to cover her actual dissatisfaction?
- What strategies of persuasion does she adopt?
- Do you think this letter is effectively written?

The editor who collected and published the Tucker family correspondence said that St. George Tucker granted Phillis's wish and sent her on to Missouri.

Document 2.12.10: James Hope's letter

- What is the stated purpose of James Hope's letter?
- What does he want his master to do for him?
- How does he appeal to Beverly to do what he wishes? Consider especially his statement that "if you will be so kind to your servant as to order him sent on your servant will ever reverence and obey his master" and his plea that his master "oblige his Jim."
- List the people Hope mentions and consider how they are related to him.
- How long does it seem that he has been separated from them and has not heard news about them? Hope's sister Francis, who is mentioned twice, was twenty-two years old in 1824; James was thirty-seven.
- Make a chart of his family and friends: his sister, father, "cozens" [cousins], godfather, and "old ecquantance" [acquaintances]. Note that, in African American kinship, cousinship was especially meaningful; sisters' and brothers' children might have close bonds. But not all "cousins" were blood relatives; "fictive kin," such as adopted aunts, uncles, and cousins, were important, especially when blood kin were separated.
- What relatives might James Hope not have mentioned in this letter?
- What might have led him not to mention his mother? Can you tell whether he had a wife and children?

The editor of the Tucker family correspondence does not say whether Beverly Tucker granted his slaves' requests.

Document 2.12.11: Susan and Ersey's letter

- Why do the women resist leaving Missouri?
- What solution do they suggest that will allow them to remain in St. Louis?
- What might the white men whom they mention be willing to do?
- How do Susan and Ersey attempt to persuade their owner to let them remain in St. Louis? Consider their statements that "we hope and pray that you will not think hard of us" for making this request and "we do not do it through any disrespect."
- How do they attempt to cover their own defiance of their master's wishes?
- What do you think they might have done if Tucker turned down their request and required them to go to Texas? Try to figure out what chance they might have had of running away to free territory.

Letter Writing—Responses from the Tuckers and Communication Between Slaves

Activity 4

After students discuss the letters, ask them to write: (1) a letter from St. George or Nathaniel Beverly Tucker in reply to a slave's letter, especially the petitions of Phillis, James Hope, or Susan and Ersey; and (2) a letter from one slave to another, which their masters would not see, when they were separated—from Phillis to her children in Missouri, for example, or from Francis in Virginia to her brother, James Hope.

Further Student and Teacher Resources

Berlin, Ira., and Leslie S. Rowland, eds. *Families and Freedom: A Documentary History of African-American Kinship in the Civil War Era.* New York: New Press, 1997.

Berlin, Ira, Marc Favreau, and Steven F. Miller, eds. *Remembering Slavery: African Americans Talk about Their Personal Experiences of Slavery and Emancipation.* With sound recordings. Published in conjunction with the Library of Congress and the Smithsonian Institution. New York: New Press, 1998.

Blassingame, John W., ed. *Slave Testimony: Two Centuries of Letters, Speeches, Interviews, and Autobiographies.* Baton Rouge: Louisiana State University Press, 1997.

Fehrenbacher, Don Edwards, completed and edited by Ward M. McAfee. *The Slaveholding Republic: An Account of the United States Government's Relation to Slavery.* New York: Oxford University Press, 2001.

> ## Contemporary Connection
> ※
>
> ### Crossroads of the Nation
>
> Missouri today offers a rich resource for the study of African American history. The tourism website describes the state as the "crossroads of the nation," the "beginning of the west, the end of the east, the top of the south and the bottom of the north." Here we read about the Missouri Compromise of 1820 and about the 1866 founding of the Lincoln Institute, a school for newly freed slaves. A good source of information on the African American history of Missouri is the Ethnic Studies Center at the Inman Page Library in Jefferson City. The Center holds special collections of black history materials and sponsors workshops and exhibits related to these materials. Kansas City is home to the Negro Leagues Baseball Museum and the Black Archives of Mid-America. Other cities, such as St. Charles and St. Louis, also have a significant African American past and present and offer numerous ways to discover that story. To begin the search, check *www.missouritourism.org*.

Fehrenbacher, Don Edwards. *The South and Three Sectional Crises*. Baton Rouge: Louisiana State University Press, 1986.

Gutman, Herbert G. *The Black Family in Slavery and Freedom*. New York: Vintage Books, 1976.

Moore, Glover. *The Missouri Compromise*. Lexington: University of Kentucky Press, 1967.

Primary Source Materials for Lesson 12

2.12.1

Excerpts from the Northwest Ordinance, July 13, 1787

Art. 5. There shall be formed in the said territory, not less than three nor more than five States; and the boundaries of the States, as soon as Virginia shall alter her act of cession, and consent to the same, shall become fixed and established as follows, to wit: The western State in the said territory, shall be bounded by the Mississippi, the Ohio, and Wabash Rivers; a direct line drawn from the Wabash and Post Vincents, due North, to the territorial line between the United States and Canada; and, by the said territorial line, to the Lake of the Woods and Mississippi. The middle State shall be bounded by the said direct line, the Wabash from Post Vincents to the Ohio, by the Ohio, by a direct line, drawn due north from the mouth of the Great Miami, to the said territorial line, and by the said territorial line. The eastern State shall be bounded by the last mentioned direct line, the Ohio, Pennsylvania, and the said territorial line: *Provided, however,* and it is further understood and declared, that the boundaries of these three States shall be subject so far to be altered, that, if Congress shall hereafter find it expedient, they shall have authority to form one or two States in that part of the said territory which lies north of an east and west line drawn through the southerly bend or extreme of Lake Michigan. And, whenever any of the said States shall have sixty thousand free inhabitants therein, such State shall be admitted, by its delegates, into the Congress of the United States, on an equal footing with the original States in all respects whatever, and shall be at liberty to form a permanent constitution and State government: *Provided,* the constitution and government so to be formed, shall be republican, and in conformity to the principles contained in these articles; and, so far as it can be consistent with the general interest of the confederacy, such admission shall be allowed at an earlier period, and when there may be a less number of free inhabitants in the State than sixty thousand.

Art. 6. There shall be neither slavery nor involuntary servitude in the said territory, otherwise than in the punishment of crimes whereof the party shall have been duly convicted: *Provided, always,* That any person escaping into the same, from whom labor or service is lawfully claimed in any one of the original States, such fugitive may be lawfully reclaimed and conveyed to the person claiming his or her labor or service as aforesaid.

The full text of Document 2.12.1. is available on the CD-ROM.

2.12.2

The Tallmadge Amendment to Missouri's application for statehood, February 13, 1819

And provided also, That the further introduction of slavery or involuntary servitude be prohibited, except for the punishment of crimes, whereof the party shall be duly convicted: and that all children of slaves, born within the said state, after the admission thereof into the Union, shall be free but may be held to service until the age of twenty-five years.

2.12.3

The Thomas Amendment to Missouri's application for statehood, February 17, 1820

And be it further enacted, That, in all that territory ceded by France to the United States under the name of Louisiana, which lies north of thirty-six degrees and thirty minutes north latitude, excepting only such part thereof as is included within the limits of the State contemplated by this act, slavery and involuntary servitude, otherwise than in the punishment of crimes whereof the party shall have been duly convicted, shall be and is hereby forever prohibited: *Provided always,* That any person escaping into the same, from whom labor or service is lawfully claimed in any State or Territory of the United States, such fugitive may be lawfully reclaimed, and conveyed to the person claiming his or her labor or service, as aforesaid.

2.12.4

Excerpts from the Missouri Enabling Act, March 6, 1820

SEC 3. That all free white male citizens of the United States, who shall have arrived at the age of twenty-one years, and have resided in said territory three months previous to the day of election, and all other persons qualified to vote for representatives to the general assembly of the said territory, shall be qualified to be elected, and they are hereby qualified and authorized to vote, and choose representatives to form a convention . . . .

SEC. 8. That in all that territory ceded by France to the United States, under the name of Louisiana, which lies north of thirty-six degrees and thirty minutes north latitude, not included within the limits of the state, contemplated by this act, slavery and involuntary servitude, otherwise than in the punishment of crimes, whereof the parties shall have been duly convicted, shall be, and is hereby, forever prohibited: *Provided always,* That any person escaping into the same, from whom labour or service is lawfully claimed, in any state or territory of the United States, such fugitive may be lawfully reclaimed and conveyed to the person claiming his or her labour or service as aforesaid.

The full text of Document 2.12.4 is available on the CD-ROM.

2.12.5

Excerpts from the Constitution of Missouri, July 19, 1820

SEC. 26. The general assembly shall not have power to pass laws—

1. For the emancipation of slaves without the consent of their owners; or without paying them, before such emancipation, a full equivalent for such slaves so emancipated; and,
2. To prevent *bona-fide* immigrants to this state, or actual settlers therein, from bringing from any of the United States, or from any of their Territories, such persons as may there be deemed to be slaves, so long as any persons of the same description are allowed to be held as slaves by the laws of this State.

They shall have power to pass laws—

1. To prevent *bona-fide* immigrants to this State from bringing into this State any slaves who may have committed any high crime in any other State or Territory;
2. To prohibit the introduction of any slave for the purpose of speculation, or as an article of trade or merchandise;
3. To prohibit the introduction of any slave, or the offspring of any slave, who heretofore may have been, or who hereafter may be, imported from any foreign country into the United States, or any Territory thereof, in contravention of any existing statute of the United States; and,
4. To permit the owners of slaves to emancipate them, saving the rights of creditors, where the person so emancipating will give security that the slave so emancipated shall not become a public charge.

It shall be their duty, as soon as may be, to pass such laws as may be necessary—

1. To prevent free negroes [and] mulattoes from coming to and settling in this State, under any pretext whatsoever; and,
2. To oblige the owners of slaves to treat them with humanity, and to abstain from all injuries to them extending to life or limb.

2.12.6

Resolution for the Admission of Missouri, March 2, 1821

Resolution providing for the admission of the State of Missouri into the Union, on a certain condition.

Resolved, That Missouri shall be admitted into this union on an equal footing with the original states, in all respects whatever, upon the fundamental condition, that the fourth clause of the twenty-sixth section of the third article of the constitution submitted on the part of said state to Congress, shall never be construed to authorize the passage of any law, and that no law shall be passed in conformity thereto, by which any citizen, of either of the states in this Union, shall be excluded from the enjoyment of any of the privileges and immunities to which such citizen is entitled under the constitution of the United States: *Provided,* That the legislature of the said state, by a solemn public act, shall declare the assent of the said state to the said fundamental condition, and shall transmit to the President of the United States, on or before the fourth Monday in November next, an authentic copy of the said act; upon the receipt whereof, the President, by proclamation, shall announce the fact; whereupon, and without any further proceeding on the part of Congress, the admission of the said state into this Union shall be considered as complete.

2.12.7

Phil Anthony's letter to St. George Tucker, September 14, 1807

I received my good master's letter of the 4th and will endeavor to have every part of it complied with. Judy's youngest Child has been sick but is getting better. Several of the servants have had ague and fever but are now about. Aleck is better but has never left town. I recd the timber to do the house on this day week and have the promise of the workman to begin it tomorrow. I have had the house whitewashed throughout and hope Ben will put it in good order for your reception.

With the timber I recd a box of loaf of sugar, two barrels of brown, a bag of Coffee and a bundle of books accompanied by a letter from Mr Waddy saying there was no such wine to be had as you wanted and that he should wait your further directions respecting it. Miss Bowdion has preserved some peaches for Mistress but Mrs Peachy waits for those in the garden which are not yet ripe. The former has been ill for several days past, and is still very sick. She desired me to send her love to you all.

The full text of Document 2.12.7 is available on the CD-ROM.

2.12.8

Cyfax Brown's letter to St. George Tucker, May 15, 1822

Prince Edward May 15th 1822

Dear Master [St. George Tucker] the 15th day of March 1781 at the Battle of Gilford I was then a man and a Servant to you: which you know: and a Gentleman you were then and I hope you are yet. I am now unable to Support my Self as I am old and infirme pray my old Master can you help the old servant in his old age to something if you please If you feel disposed to send me Something you can Lodg it with nick Scott my nephew in Richmond then I can get it Seartinley

Your most humble Servant
Cyfax Brown

2.12.9

Phillis' letter to Mr. and Mrs. St. George Tucker, 1824

Loveing Master and Mistress [Mr. and Mrs. St. George Tucker]. I take the Lebberties of informing you of my present wishes of which I hope you will not Be Displeased at nor think that I am not Satisfied with my Situation of Life—So far from that it gave me pleasure to say that you Boath have discharge your duty to me as any Servant have any Right to Expect or wish for—But old age And infirmity Begins to follow me which Cause me to think that my Business in Life are nealy to an End—tho I know From my heart that you and Mistress would never See me Suffer as long as my Body Lives and you Live But I am going down very fast to my grave and if you please By your Premitions Boath you and Mistress I would go and Live those other few dais with master Beverly and my Children

From your Servant Phillis

2.12.10

James Hope's letter to Mr. Beverly Tucker, November 16, 1834

Dr Master [Beverly Tucker]

your servant James is also desirous of returning to his place of Nativity and if you (Master) should return in the spring if you will be so kind to your servant as to order him sent on your servant will ever reverence and obey his master your James wishes you to read this to his old eqcuantance to all of which he wishes to be remembered and particularly Gaberil Toney Benjamin King your Servant James also would inform his Master that he together with his fallow Servants are getting along peacible and in a way that he hopes will afford Master pleasure when he may see cause to return to Missouri if Master cannot make it convenient to see my sister he will oblige his Jim by Inclosing this to my sister and she will see the principal object of this has been to inquire after I hope she answer my inquiries herself

from you obt Servant
James Hope

The full text of Document 2.12.10 is available on the CD-ROM.

2.12.11

Susan (Sukey) and Ersey's letter to Mr. Beverly Tucker, October 24, 1842

Dear Master [Beverly Tucker]—

We, two of your humble Servants have come to the conclusion to write you a few lines upon a subject that has given us much pain, which will be more keenly felt if you will not grant their humble request. We hope and pray that you will not think hard of us in so doing, as we are in much distress, and write the very feelings of our hearts.

About two weeks ago Mr Jones, a neighbor of Mr Bundlett in Texas, called with a letter from Mr Bundlett saying that we must come on with Mr Jones. As we had been here a long time and had become much attached to the place (our Husbands being here) and as we hated the idea of going to Texas, Mr Jones was kind enough to let us remain till March, before which time he expected to hear from you on the subject. Our object in writing dear Master is this: We can't bear to go to Texas with a parcel of strangers— if you were there we should go without saying a word, but to be separated from our husbands forever in this world would make us unhappy for life. We have a great many friends in this place and would rather be sold than go to Texas . . . .

The full text of Document 2.12.11 is available on the CD-ROM.

Glossary

abettors: those who encourage and support another person, usually one who is breaking the law.

able-bodied: robust, fit for physical service; in the merchant marine, an ordinary seaman who is trained and/or experienced.

accommodation: the act of doing a favor for or compromising with another person or group; also, giving lodgings or providing a convenience to another.

adherence: the state of being attached or devoted to a position, person, or faith.

affidavit: a sworn, written declaration made before a legal authority.

almanac: an annual calendar, giving the days, weeks, and months of the year, weather forecasts, astronomical information, times of high and low tides, the best times to plant and harvest crops and, often, miscellaneous advice.

amendment: a change in a document, such as a motion, bill, or constitution; also, an improvement or correction of a fault.

appeal: to ask for aid from a higher authority; to request that a legal case be reheard by a higher court.

apprentice: a young person bound to serve a master for a term of years in order to learn a skilled trade; under programs for the gradual abolition of slavery in the early nineteenth century, a formerly enslaved person to be freed after serving a term of years; after Emancipation, an ex-slave bound to work for a set term and forbidden to contract freely with another employer.

attorney: a person empowered to represent another person in legal matters.

bark (barque): a sailing ship with three or more masts that are fore-and-aft rigged—that is, square-rigged on all but the mizzenmast.

battalion: a military unit consisting of two or more companies or, more generally, any large body of troops.

bicameral parliament or legislature: a legislative body with two chambers, houses, or branches, such as (in Britain) a House of Lords and House of Commons or (in the United States) a Senate and House of Representatives.

boatsteerer: someone who steers a boat, a small, open watercraft; on a whaling ship, the harpooner.

bootblacker (bootblack): someone who polishes, or "blacks," boots and shoes.

brethren: members of a brotherhood, often a religious group; the male members of a group, referred to collectively.

brig (short for brigantine): a two-masted ship, square-rigged on both masts, sometimes carrying a spanker.

brig: a place of confinement on shipboard, similar to a prison cell.

caste: any distinct social group in which membership is based on heredity.

census: an official count of the inhabitants of a country or state, with information about the inhabitants' age, sex, race, etc.

chattel: a form of slavery in which persons are owned by others and can be bought, sold, and bequeathed as if they were property; a movable article of personal property distinct from real estate.

civil suit: a legal action brought by one person against another, as distinct from a criminal prosecution, in which the government brings charges against a person.

civilized: enlightened, educated, and refined, contrasted with a state of savagery or barbarism; often used to assert the superiority of Europeans over Africans and Native Americans or advocated as a program of imposing European culture on those groups.

coastal: of, at, near, or pertaining to the seashore, where land meets ocean.

colonization: the act of establishing people born in one place to live in another place, which remains under the control of their country of origin, regardless of who the original inhabitants of that place were; in the early nineteenth century, the proposal or practice of sending free persons of African descent to specific places in Africa, where they would speak English, encourage other people to convert to Christianity, and spread European American values.

confiscation: the act of taking property, done by governmental authority, sometimes converting it to public use or profit, often as punishment for a crime.

conspiracy: a secret plot or plan to accomplish some end, usually an illegal one.

cooper: a skilled artisan who makes and repairs wooden containers, such as casks, barrels, and buckets.

crescendo of expectations: a process by which a group's expectations, hopes, or apprehensions increase over time, which can become self-perpetuating and/or lead to a crisis.

cross-reference: a system of noting what parts of a document refer or pertain to other parts of that or another document; a note directing a reader to another part of a book or document.

deep-sea: (adjective) of or pertaining to the ocean, as distinct from coastal or inland waterways.

depose: (verb) to deprive a person of his rank or office, to oust or overthrow an official.

depose and testify: to give written or oral testimony in a legal case.

deposition: sworn testimony taken outside a court of law, used in court when oral testimony cannot be obtained.

dichotomy: a division between two branches, sections, or aspects of a matter; a division into mutually exclusive and often opposed parts.

discharge: to remove by unloading; to fire a weapon; to dismiss from office or employment; to release or set at liberty, as a prisoner or patient; to perform, fulfill, or complete a duty, responsibility, or trust; to pay a debt or satisfy an obligation; to set aside legally, to annul.

durante vita: for their entire life.

emancipation: the act of releasing from slavery, bondage, or servitude.

endow: to furnish or equip, as with natural talents or gifts.

estate: one's entire property or possessions, especially of a deceased person; a large piece of land with a residence.

faculty: a natural or acquired ability to do something, a special aptitude or skill; one of the powers inherent in body and/or mind, such a speaking or seeing.

foc's'cle (forecastle): that part of the upper deck of a ship forward of the mast nearest the bow, where sailors' living quarters are located.

forfeiture: the act of giving up or losing something as a penalty, or that which is given up as the penalty fixed for an offense, crime, or error.

genealogy: the practice of tracing one's ancestry as far back as possible; a chart of all those directly descended from a progenitor.

greenhand (green hand): a person who is new at an occupation, lacking the expertise that comes from experience.

greenhorn: a newly arrived immigrant; one who is easily duped.

guinea: an English coin, issued from 1663 to 1813, once equal to 21 shillings (one shilling more than a pound sterling), so called because the gold used to make it came from the African country of Guinea.

habeas corpus: a writ requiring a person who detains another to produce that person for a court hearing, usually to determine whether the person is being held lawfully; literally, "you have the body"; a basic right under English and American law.

harpooner: the highly skilled member of a whaleboat crew who throws the harpoon, a long, barbed lance attached with a line that strikes and secures the whale.

head of household: the person who represents and acts for a household, a group of persons who reside together, in public or civil society; formerly the adult male who was regarded as controlling his wife, children, other dependents, servants, and/or slaves.

"His Majesty's tenders": the King's offers.

"hue and cry": the pursuit of a felon with loud shouts and outcries, all who heard being legally obliged to join the search.

imprudence: the quality of acting unwisely or indiscreetly.

impudence: offensive boldness of speech or action, insolence, disrespect to a person in authority.

inalienable: not transferable, that is, cannot be given or taken away or sold.

indictment: legally, a formal, written charge of crime, prosecuted by the government and brought by a grand jury as the basis for a trial; more generally, an accusation of an offense.

iniquitous: unjust; violating a right; wrongful.

insurrection: a rebellion, generally armed, against established authority.

inventory: a list of articles, with their description, quantity, and value, often the possessions of a deceased person.

investiture: the act or ceremony of giving a person the power of an office, authority, or right; the act of providing or endowing a person with qualities or traits.

law of nature: something that cannot be changed because it is inherent in the order of things; part of a theory that rights are grounded in invariable laws established by nature and/or nature's god.

lay: (noun) in whaling, a seaman's share of the profits from the voyage.

legal challenge: a strategy of trying to change a law, policy, or situation by bringing a court case against it.

manumission: the legal act of freeing one's slave.

marginalize: to treat as unimportant; to relegate to a peripheral position.

martial law: temporary rule or jurisdiction by the military forces over citizens, suspending some rights guaranteed under civil law; generally proclaimed in times of civil disorder or war.

merit-based: based on worth, excellence, or quality rather than on factors such as race, money, kinship, or favoritism.

mulatto: any person of mixed European and African descent; less commonly, persons of mixed African and Native American descent.

nation-building: the process of creating a functioning nation-state with a government, code of laws, etc.

natural rights: the rights with which people are thought to be endowed by nature.

objectified: made into a thing; for persons, treated as if one were an inanimate object.

oppression: the state of being kept down by cruel or unjust use of power or authority, often by force; the state of being crushed, trampled upon, or weighed down.

oppressor: a person who oppresses another person, holding them in subjection unjustly and by force.

partus sequitur patrem: to follow the condition of the father.

partus sequitur ventrem: to follow the condition of the mother.

pension: a fixed income allowed to a person who has retired from an office or position, often in the military.

petition: a formal request addressed to a person in authority asking for some grant or benefit or a change in something thought to be wrong, usually brought by a group of persons.

plaintiff: the person who brings a civil suit against another person (known as the defendant) or brings a legal action or complaint against some authority.

plethora: a superabundance or excess.

preamble: an introductory statement to a formal document, usually explaining its purpose and justification.

prejudice: a judgment or opinion formed beforehand, without knowledge or due consideration; bias; a negative opinion based on ignorance or irrationality; unfounded hatred of a particular racial, ethnic, or religious group.

proclamation: a formal public announcement or declaration made by a person in authority.

protocol: generally, the proper way of doing something; the rules governing the behavior of diplomats and representatives of states.

pur autre vie: for the term of their life.

ratification: the act of approving or confirming a document, action, or decision through a formal, public process.

ratify: to approve or confirm a document, action, or decision through a formal, public process.

rebellion: an armed uprising against established authority.

recruit: (verb) to induce a person to join the armed forces or another group; (noun) a person who has recently joined the armed forces or another group.

regiment: a military unit larger than a battalion and smaller than a division.

royal charter: a document issued by a King or Queen granting special rights and privileges to a group or organization, such as a colony or business company.

schooner: a ship with two or more masts rigged fore-and-aft.

ship's stewards: persons responsible for the provisions given to the crew and passengers on a ship.

solemn oath: a formal declaration, affirmation, or pledge, usually made in the name of God.

status: the accepted social position or condition of a person or group; rank relative to other persons or groups.

statute: a law created by legislation, as distinct from common law created through legal decisions.

stipulation: something that is specified as the terms of an agreement or contract.

tenets: articles of belief.

traitor: a person who betrays his or her country or government, who commits treason.

transcript: an accurate, written copy of a document or speech.

treason: betraying one's country, often to a foreign government; usually a capital offense.

try-works: the equipment, tools, etc., used to "try out," or extract, the oil from whale blubber, done on board a whaling ship.

uprising: an armed insurrection of a group of subordinated persons against their oppressive condition.

warned out: told officially to leave town, so that if a poor person remains in the local community he or she will not be entitled to receive public charity.

whale boat: a deep rowboat approximately 30 feet long, with pointed ends, that is carried on the deck of a whaling ship and launched to chase and catch whales and tow them back to the ship.

whaler: a whaling ship, or a person who works on a whaling ship.

witness: a person who testifies, usually in court, about what he or she has seen and heard.

Credits

Documents 2.1.6 A and B: Courtesy of Massachusetts Archives.

Documents 2.1.7 A and B, 2.2.22, 2.10.4, 2.11.3, 2.11.8: Courtesy of the Library of Congress.

Document 2.2.9: Courtesy of Pennsylvania Sons of the Revolution.

Document 2.2.12: Courtesy of Lafayette College Art Collection, Easton, PA.

Document 2.2.13: Courtesy of Lafayette College Special Collections & Archives.

Documents 2.2.16 and 2.7.5: Courtesy of the National Archives.

Document 2.2.20: *The Colored Patriots of the American Revolution* by William Cooper Nell.

Document 2.2.21: Courtesy of Corbis Images.

Document 2.3.7: Courtesy of Nova Scotia Archives & Records Management.

Document 2.5.1: Courtesy of Massachusetts Historical Society.

Document 2.6.3: Courtesy of Bienecke Library, Yale University.

Document 2.7.1: Courtesy of Nantucket Historical Association.

Document 2.7.4: Courtesy of New Bedford Whaling Museum.

Documents 2.12.7, 2.12.8, 2.12.9, and 2.12.11: From *Slave Testimony: Two Centuries of Letters, Speeches, Interviews, and Autobiographies,* edited by John W. Blassingame. Published by Louisiana State University Press, 1977. Reprinted by permission of the publisher.